'Becoming a mother – matrescence – involves major change – physical, psycho-logical and social. Contrary to a widespread belief, mental health problems in preg-nancy and after delivery are common, affecting approximately one in five women. The problems range from severe distress to frank psychosis. They impact not just the mother but many others, particularly the baby, partner and wider family. Most women with perinatal mental health problems will benefit from counselling. In her book, Dr Sultana provides a roadmap for therapists and other professionals working with women who are experiencing mental health problems. She shares the findings of her PhD to illuminate the themes that predominate including those that are specific to the perinatal period. The book will be a useful resource for the many professionals working in perinatal mental health.'

John Sheehan, MB, BCh, BAO, DO, DCh, FRCPI, MRCPsych, MMedSc, MCPsychI, *is a medical doctor who has worked as a consultant perinatal psychiatrist at the Rotunda Hospital since 1995. He is an Associate Clinical Professor in the UCD School of Medicine. He has a special interest in teaching and psychotherapy and was a Board member of the School of Psychotherapy at St Vincent's University Hospital.*

T0383766

Integrative Perinatal Counselling

This book presents "the Becoming Model", an integrative perinatal counselling model that provides a practical clinical framework to therapists working with those for whom the question of becoming a parent seems central.

Becoming a parent changes your identity, household, worldviews, relationships, priorities and previous life goals. Based on the notion that one does not become a mother or a father overnight, rather that it is a process of "becoming", this model provides a roadmap for therapists (psychoanalytic, behavioural, humanistic, integrative and others) looking to understand and explore their client's experience of this transitional journey through talk-therapy. It defines the unique field of perinatal counselling, highlights major clinical considerations, presents clinical observations by drawing from real-life cases and provides the therapist with one-stop-information guides on each theme (ten) and sub-theme (40) by drawing from existing research, i.e., evidence-based practice.

Arguably one of the few counselling models specific to the perinatal period, this user-friendly guide, which is applicable to any modality, is designed to support psychotherapists, counsellors, nurses, midwives and other mental health professionals working therapeutically with those who are going through the pre- or perinatal period, or those who have experienced perinatal loss.

Mou Sultana, PhD, works as a Counselling Psychologist (CPsychol, BPS) and Psychotherapist (UKCP, MICP) in private practice Need2talk and with Vhi. She is a lecturer and supervisor at the Irish College of Humanities and Applied Sciences. She specialises in perinatal mental health, sexuality, domestic violence, trauma and neuroscience.

Integrative Perinatal Counselling

The Becoming Model

Mou Sultana

Routledge
Taylor & Francis Group

LONDON AND NEW YORK

Designed cover image: © Getty Images

First published 2024
by Routledge
4 Park Square, Milton Park, Abingdon, Oxon OX14 4RN

and by Routledge
605 Third Avenue, New York, NY 10158

Routledge is an imprint of the Taylor & Francis Group, an informa business

British Library Cataloguing-in-Publication Data
A catalogue record for this book is available from the British Library

Library of Congress Cataloging-in-Publication Data
Names: Sultana, Mou, author.
Title: Integrative perinatal counselling : the becoming model / Mou Sultana.
Description: Abingdon, Oxon ; New York, NY : Routledge, 2024. |
Includes bibliographical references and index. |
Identifiers: LCCN 2023030714 (print) | LCCN 2023030715 (ebook) |
ISBN 9781032314327 (hbk) | ISBN 9781032314303 (pbk) |
ISBN 9781003309710 (ebk)
Subjects: LCSH: Pregnancy--Psychological aspects. | Perinatology. |
Childbirth--Psychological aspects. | Motherhood.
Classification: LCC RG560 .S838 2024 (print) | LCC RG560 (ebook) |
DDC 618.2--dc23/eng/20231010
LC record available at https://lccn.loc.gov/2023030714
LC ebook record available at https://lccn.loc.gov/2023030715

ISBN: 978-1-032-31432-7 (hbk)
ISBN: 978-1-032-31430-3 (pbk)
ISBN: 978-1-003-30971-0 (ebk)

DOI: 10.4324/9781003309710

Typeset in Times New Roman
by KnowledgeWorks Global Ltd.

To Ena, Isa and Violet for teaching me the essential elements of becoming a mother...

Contents

Introduction

Introduction

Perinatal mental health is a specialised field of health care that has emerged in the last decade. Perinatal Counselling and Psychotherapy is a distinct field of clinical practice that has remained severely underdeveloped in Ireland and abroad. This field requires specialist knowledge and training. The Becoming model fills this gap. With 10 major themes and 40 sub-themes, this model provides the therapist with a much need structure for conducting perinatal counselling. Any qualified therapist regardless of their school of training can use this model. Hence the main audience of this book is therapist or allied health professionals who engage in talk therapy with perinatal clients. The following sections will introduce the topic and provide an overview of the structure of this book.

"One-stop-shop"

Every therapist is an individual human being with their own preferences, training and expertise coming from diverse backgrounds and experiences. Persons attending therapy are also unique individuals with unique sets of experiences, needs and historical context. Hence, each therapeutic session is unique in its own way. The therapist's exploration style of the themes of this book will vary widely due to several unique sets of factors in play. This book does not aim to be prescriptive or predictive. However, if the therapist chooses to do so, they can use each chapter as a road map to guide their sessions. They can use the definitions and literature highlighted in each chapter as a starting point of discussion with their clients. They can also use the information as a common ground or as generally accepted facts and invite their clients to explore the themes and sub-themes in a non-judgemental and safe space guided by their clinical judgement. To facilitate this ease of use, each chapter is dedicated to a particular theme and its sub-themes. They are written in a way that they have the potential to be used as a "one-stop-shop" by the therapists. Each chapter explores a theme and its sub-themes by providing clear rationale for the inclusion of the theme in the model, noting definitions of the major terms and its related terminologies, outlining snippets of the most relevant recent/

DOI: 10.4324/9781003309710-1

current literature from wide sources including governmental guidelines and academic literature on the topic, highlighting the most crucial clinical considerations and clinical observations using real-life examples of cases.

Disproportionate expectation

"Becoming a mother/father/parent" is often glorified in the media, especially the portrayal of the perinatal period. Commercial advertisements seem to gloss over the harsh reality of this period. For instance, advertisements that are targeted to sell baby and maternity products such as nappies, clothing, furniture and equipment tend to portray a happy and content-looking mom/dad with freshly washed hair rocking a calmly sleeping baby. When in reality it is a sleep-deprived parent who can barely find clothes that do not have baby spit on them. They probably have not had a chance to wash their hair for a few days. They are probably desperately trying to find ways to soothe their babies who are screaming their lungs out due to colic! But such a picture will not be approved by the marketing teams as it will not help sell packets of nappies. The expectation of life with new babies is hence disproportionate to reality. Clinical experience has taught us that this is anything but a safe and calm period. As a rule of thumb one can consider that if a person is about to have ten instances of psychological difficulties in their lifetime, they are probably going to have seven to eight of those instances in their perinatal period. This is because becoming a parent is one of the most significant and life-changing events. Similarly, over 80% of couples are going to have some sort of abusive exchange with one another during this period. Furthermore, 100% of couples are going to have at least some levels of disagreements, arguments and fights during this period. The glorification of this period thus simply creates expectations that are far from reality. However, this book sincerely hopes not to put anyone off having children!

In the making...

Often what a new parent complains about the most is exhaustion. They are also often frustrated. This is primarily because they are constantly trying to keep on top of everything. They try to juggle being a mom/dad/parent to their other children, a partner to one another, an employee to their boss and colleagues, a friend, a neighbour, a cousin, a sibling, an adult child to their own parents and also a parent to their new child. In the exploration of these multiple roles in therapy what often comes to surface is that they feel guilt from complaining; feel guilty from not keeping calm; for believing that they are not doing it "right" compared to "other parents". Their anger/frustration is often misdirected and misplaced. They begin to consciously realise in therapy that they are trying to achieve something that is impossible to achieve. In most cases, they also realise that in this process of trying to achieve everything "right", they have forgotten how to be a partner! Unfortunately, the one role and in most cases the first role that most parents sacrifice or forget to maintain is the relationship with their partner(s) after the arrival of a baby. Many of those parents (with/without partners) also forget, how to be themselves! Reconnecting with one's partner and redefining the emerging new version of one's self are the most common latent themes that come to surface in therapy when exploring distress and difficulties experienced during the perinatal period. This is a transitionary period. People's lives undergo changes and transformations during this period. Like a construction site, this period is messy! But only because the future is under construction, the future is being built!

The Becoming model has 10 major themes and 40 sub-themes. Each chapter explores a theme and its related sub-themes. However, the model does not have exhaustion, guilt, frustration and anger as separate themes in this model. Instead, they are considered to be omnipresent in every theme. These terms are scattered throughout the book and more directly discussed in the following chapters: Exhaustion is mentioned in Chapter 11 under "Previous diagnosis" and in Chapter 13 under "Support". Guilt, frustration and anger are explored under "Aggression" in Chapter 8 and Chapter 12.

Diversity and inclusivity

The pronouns used in this book aimed to be inclusive. However, the book uses the phrase "mother/father/parent" to denote the perinatal client. The book also uses the phrase "becoming a mother" on several occasions. This is not meant to be exclusive to female-bodied persons. Moreover, the book may seem to be highlighting the experience of "becoming a mother/father/parent" for the first time. This model is not restrictive to first-time parents. The phrase "Becoming a parent" is meant to be inclusive of all parents. In that sense, it is meant to include situations such as "becoming a parent again". The model is therefore also applicable to parents with multiple children. This is because becoming a parent at different stages in life, to different children, is a unique experience. Navigating one's own relationship with partner(s) or other significant other(s) is also unique during these periods. Hence, each pregnancy, each birth and each child can be a different experience. The phrase "becoming a mother/father/parent" is meant to include previous and subsequent pregnancy, birth and children. In that sense, the phrase "becoming a mother/father/ parent again" is more appropriate. But this phrase has not been used throughout. The "Becoming model" is thus not restricted to a first-time parent or a single-child family.

Moreover, this book at times may seem to be written from a perspective of a heterosexual couple who have had a live healthy birth. This is not meant to be the case. The model is not aimed at couples only. The couple does not have to be heterosexual. They also do not have to have a live birth for this model to be applied to their case in therapeutic settings. They may be heterosexual and/or same sex. They may also be from a diverse relationship background such as polyamorous or open relationship. They may also be a single mother/parent/carer rearing the child with the help of a family member or a friend or someone else with whom they may or may not have sexual relationship. This model is not restricted to traditional relationships only. They may have also been struggling to conceive, have not conceived, experienced pregnancy loss, may have experienced stillbirth or may have lost the child during their perinatal period. They also do not have to have a healthy child for this model to be applicable. The child could be unwell at birth, unwell throughout the perinatal period, deteriorating gradually, hospitalised, may have a disability or health condition, may have a fussy personality or may be a child who just will not settle for any other reason. The "Becoming model" is applicable to all of these situations. However, this book should be only used by qualified therapists or allied health professionals who engage in talk therapy. While the "Becoming model" provides the therapists with a structure or a road map for their therapy sessions, their work should always be guided by their clinical judgment.

Chapter 1

Definition and Scope

Introduction

Perinatal mental health refers to mental health during the perinatal period. Perinatal counselling refers to professionals engaging therapeutically in the forms of counselling and psychotherapy with perinatal clients. This chapter provides some context about the topic, highlights some high-level views of prevalence, outlines the definitions of some of the major terminologies relevant to this topic, defines the perinatal period and perinatal counselling, clarifies the criteria for considering someone as a perinatal client for counselling and finally defines the scope of the Becoming model.

Context

What comes to mind when you hear the phrase "perinatal mental health"? The general population may not be familiar with this term. Professionals too may not be quite familiar with the phrase unless they have previous knowledge of this field and/or they work within the health and allied healthcare industry. Among professionals within the field, postnatal depression (PND) or postpartum depression (PPD) is the most common association one makes in relation to the topic of perinatal mental health. It can be argued that this is the most common association among people both within and outside the professional world. This book will confirm that the perinatal period is much more than PND. The general assumption made by most people when discussing this topic is that this field is mainly relevant to women. Particularly, women who have or are about to have children. This book will clarify that this field is relevant to everyone despite their gender and the presence or absence of a baby. Another general assumption about this field among both lay and professional people is that mental health difficulties related to the perinatal period occur immediately or soon after birth but not later. Clinical experiences negate this assumption too. In other words, PND is not the only psychological difficulty experienced by someone during the perinatal period. There are a number of different types of distress and disorder that a person can experience during the perinatal period. This period does not only affect women, men too

DOI: 10.4324/9781003309710-2

can be impacted by perinatal mental health difficulties. In addition, the difficulties do not occur only soon after or around birth. They can occur anytime during or before pregnancy and can also occur much after birth such as a year postpartum or much later. However, PND, which is arguably the only term that is colloquially used to refer to the distress experienced by people in their perinatal period, is not a term that is used in the Diagnostic Statistical Manual (DSM) (American Psychiatric Association [APA], 2017). In other words, PND is a colloquial term, not a diagnostic term in the DSM. The following is a snippet from a recent study summarising the mention of PND and other relevant terms in the DSM (Baldoni & Giannotti, 2020).

> Although these terms are commonly used in research, these diagnoses are not even mentioned in the current DSM-5. The manual only specifies the criteria for a major depressive episode "with peripartum onset" referring to the mother only, which is defined as the most recent episode occurring during pregnancy as well as in the 4 weeks following delivery.

The Becoming model goes much beyond the DSM's description of PND. Precisely because both research-based practice and practice-based research would confirm that most perinatal mental health difficulties and distress experienced within this period are usually much beyond the narrow set of criteria outlined in the DSM. However, PND is conceptualised by the APA as a mental disorder. For any mental disorder to be screened, assessed, diagnosed and treated, there needs to be a distinct set of criteria and symptoms that most professionals can agree to *use*. However, professionals do not necessarily have to agree on the ontological and phenomenological background of the classifications. Hence, the DSM's definition is very much needed and has its own place within the landscape of mental health, perhaps the centre stage for a number of reasons that are beyond the scope of this book to critique. However, it is essential that clinicians have their own positions in relation to the philosophy behind and the usage of the terminologies such as difficulties, distress, mental health, ill health, conditions, disorders, illness and so on when working therapeutically in this field. I have explored these distinctions elsewhere (Sultana, 2021, pp. 22–23) and will only outline the terminologies that are used in this book: Perinatal mental health difficulties, perinatal distress, perinatal mental disorder, serious mental illness. The following sections are aimed at providing some basic prevalence rates, definitions of these and some more relevant terms and highlight the scope of this model.

Prevalence

The National Health Service (NHS), a publicly funded healthcare system of the United Kingdom (UK) clarified, "One in five women will experience a mental health problem during their pregnancy and in the first year after birth, with depression and anxiety disorders being the most common" (NHS, 2019). The Health Services Executive, a similar public body in Ireland, outlined their specialist perinatal mental health services in the following way (HSE, 2023).

> Although as many as 1 in 5 women have mental health problems in pregnancy or after birth a perinatal mental health service will usually look after someone who has a more serious or complex mental health problem. So, not every woman with a mental health problem during pregnancy, or after their baby is born, will need this service.

The prevalence of perinatal mental health difficulties is high: **One in five**. However, not every difficulties require visits to the specialist perinatal mental health services. The following are snippets outlining the prevalences of the major mental health difficulties within the Irish context that one might experience published in the official document titled the *Specialist Perinatal Mental Health Services: Model of Care* (HSE, 2017).

> 10-15% of women suffer from mild to moderate postnatal depression. Most can be managed in primary care with access to specialist advice. 3% of women, again postnatally, suffer from moderate to severe mental health illness and require referral to secondary mental healthcare services. Of this cohort, one third would benefit from direct care and treatment from a specialist perinatal mental health service.
>
> 2/1000 women delivered are likely to suffer from a postnatal psychosis, most of whom will require inpatient treatment. Another 2/1000 delivered may suffer from serious/complex disorders, some of whom may also require inpatient treatment …
>
> Post-traumatic Stress Disorder is estimated to occur in up to 3% of maternities and 6% of women following emergency caesarean section.
>
> Finally, whilst childbirth is expected to be a time of great joy, it is not unusual for it to cause emotional upheaval with difficulties in adjusting to changes in lifestyle and relationships. This of itself can lead to adjustment disorders with significant distress for the new mother …

The major types of difficulties that one might experience during the perinatal period are mentioned below from the Irish context.

Significant definitions

The following are terms that are mentioned in this book and are essential for the discussion on perinatal mental health. It is always best practice to be guided by the guidelines published by the NHS of the country one practices in. This book is written mainly based on clinical experiences carried out in Ireland. Hence, the following terms are defined using the Irish health services guidelines.

Baby Blues: This is usually a response to hormonal and physical changes postpartum but does not stay for long, "usually begin on day 3 after your baby has been born. As your body starts to return to normal, these feelings pass" (HSE, 2023).

PND: This is usually similar to the condition of major depressive disorder (MDD) described in the DSM-5 (APA, 2017) and developed within the perinatal period, "can start at any point in the first year after giving birth and may develop suddenly or gradually" (HSE, 2023).

Postnatal Psychosis: Postnatal or puerperal psychosis is "a rare and severe form of postnatal depression ... happens within the first few weeks after giving birth. It can begin as early as 2 to 3 days after childbirth" (HSE, 2023).

PPD in men: MDD can also be experienced by men during the perinatal period. The prevalence varies from 8–10% to 18%. **One or two in ten** men will experience PND. The following is a snippet of a significant study published in Innovations in Clinical Neuroscience (Scarff, 2019).

> There are no established criteria for PPD in men, although it could present over the course of a year, with symptoms of irritability restricted emotions, and depression. Risk factors include a history of depression in either parent, poverty, and hormonal changes ... approximately 8 to 10 percent of fathers, PPD has the highest prevalence within 3 to 6 months postpartum but might insidiously develop over a year rather than four weeks postpartum ... In a review of 43 multinational studies, up to 18 percent of postpartum men reported high levels of anxiety that did not meet criteria for a specific anxiety disorder.

Mental health: This book used this term with a similar meaning outlined by the World Health Organisation (WHO, 2022).

> ... a state of mental well-being that enables people to cope with the stresses of life, realize their abilities, learn well and work well, and contribute to their community ... integral component of health and well-being that underpins our individual and collective abilities to make decisions, build relationships and shape the world we live in ... a basic human right ... crucial to personal, community and socio-economic development ... is more than the absence of mental disorders ... exists on a complex continuum, which is experienced differently from one person to the next, with varying degrees of difficulty and distress and potentially very different social and clinical outcomes.

Wellbeing: This term is used in this book in the same sense as the APA dictionary outlined it, "a state of happiness and contentment, with low levels of distress, overall good physical and mental health and outlook, or good quality of life" (APA, 2023).

Perinatal wellbeing: This term is used in the same meaning as "wellbeing" mentioned above but within the context of the perinatal period.

Perinatal mental health difficulties: An umbrella term used in this book to encompass psychological distress and disorders including depression and anxiety emerged and re-emerged during the perinatal period both diagnosed and undiagnosed.

Perinatal distress: Same meaning as "distress" or "psychological distress", except within the context of the perinatal period only. This is a similar umbrella term to perinatal mental health difficulties. Sometimes referred to as maternal distress. The term "distress" in this book is also used the same way as the APA Dictionary defined it (APA, 2023), except the term is used here within the context of the perinatal period.

> … the negative stress response, often involving negative affect and physiological reactivity: a type of stress that results from being overwhelmed by demands, losses, or perceived threats. It has a detrimental effect by generating physical and psychological maladaptation and posing serious health risks for individuals. This generally is the intended meaning of the word stress

This is an all-encompassing term that includes psychological difficulties such as stress, panic, anxiety and depression. Button et al. (2017) published their meta-synthetic study in the British Journal of General Practice on this term and defined it in the following way:

> The concept of perinatal psychological distress is not well defined in the literature, but is closely linked to stress and coping. Although some stressors may be adaptive, psychological distress, generally, involves a maladaptive psychological response to a demand. This creates an adverse emotional state, which may be reflected in a person's behaviour, possibly causing them 'harm', for example, by adversely affecting interpersonal relationships … encompasses a range of psychological symptoms, such as anxiety, stress, and depression, arising from a variety of stressors.

Perinatal mental disorder: This term is used in this book as having the same meaning as "mental disorder", except within the context of the perinatal period. The term "mental disorder" in this book is also used the same way as the APA Dictionary defined it (APA, 2023).

> any condition characterized by cognitive and emotional disturbances, abnormal behaviors, impaired functioning, or any combination of these. Such disorders cannot be accounted for solely by environmental circumstances and may involve physiological, genetic, chemical, social, and other factors. Specific classifications of mental disorders are elaborated in the American Psychiatric Association's Diagnostic and Statistical Manual of Mental Disorders

(see DSM–IV–TR; DSM–5) and the World Health Organization's International Classification of Diseases. Also called **mental illness; psychiatric disorder; psychiatric illness; psychological disorder**

Serious mental illness: This term is used in this book as having the same meaning as "mental disorder".

Defining the perinatal period and perinatal counselling

How do we define the "perinatal period"? The perinatal period itself can be described in several ways. The exact definition of this period varies among both inter-disciplines and intra-disciplines. The WHO (2016) works with the following definition, "the perinatal period commences at 22 completed weeks (154 days) of gestation and ends seven completed days after birth". The Australian Government (Australian Institute of Health and Welfare, 2005) "for the purposes of perinatal data collection" recommends that their services consider the perinatal period as commencing "at 20 completed weeks (140 days) of gestation and ends 28 completed days after birth". Both definitions have a significant difference in terms of the ending of the perinatal period. This is of particular interest considering that general statistics within the perinatal mental health research suggest that the development or onset of psychiatric disorders or relapse in case of prior history of psychiatric disorders may occur during the time of pregnancy and during the first two years post delivery. Hence, McGrandles and Duffy (2012, p. 35) suggested that the term "perinatal mental health" encompasses "the various mental health disorders experienced by women during pregnancy and the postnatal period". This is because, according to Johnson et al. (2012) and Austin et al. (2008) perinatal mental health disorder is experienced by one in five women within the first year after the birth of the baby. This statistic is even applicable to women who have never been screened, diagnosed or undergone treatment (Johnson et al. 2012; Austin et al., 2008). Hence, what seems really important to consider from a counselling psychotherapy context is that the perinatal period is conceptualised with an extended finishing line that goes beyond the first year of birth of the baby.

McGrandles and Duffy (2012, p. 25) thus highlighted that the length of the perinatal period varies across literature where some might consider it as lasting from the conception to the end of the first year post delivery and others might extend it to two years post birth. The Royal College of Psychiatrists (RCPsych, 2021) considers perinatal psychiatry as a special branch which offers specialist services to women during the perinatal period "defined as pregnancy until the end of the first postnatal year" and in some cases women may receive "continued access to specialist support into the second postnatal year". They further outline that they also help during the pre-conception period, such as those "planning a first pregnancy, or who already has children and wants to get pregnant again " (RCPsych, 2018). RCPsych's guidelines expand the scope of the perinatal team and arguably by virtue expands the perinatal period to even before conception. Considering the RCPsych's definition and scope, it is further advised that within the counselling psychotherapy context perinatal period is conceptualised with an extended starting point as before conception. This would suggest that there is an overlap between the extended perinatal period proposed here and the field of fertility counselling.

Fertility counselling generally involves exploring options of becoming a parent and emotions around potential parenthood, including "grief and loss, options and implications of assisted reproduction, using donor eggs or sperm, exploring surrogacy options" (IFCA, 2022). The psychological field irrespective of the modality (psychoanalytic, cognitive-behavioural, humanistic and so on) would univocally agree on the fact that the human mind is one of the most complex entities on this planet and it does not automatically function rationally. In fact, most automatic functioning of the human mind observed in clinical settings are seen as problematic and irrational. Within the field of perinatal mental health, clinical experience has taught us that the presence or absence of a baby does not really determine the course of one's psychological mechanism. How? Let us consider the cooling situation. A baby sucks its thumb to soothe itself. The thumb is not food. The baby does not receive nutrients by sucking it. Yet the baby receives something from that sucking and it continues. The sucking fulfils something inside that child for it to repeat itself. It can be argued that the child imagines its thumb as a substitution for the breast or the bottle. In that case, technically this can be considered as hallucination as this act involves imagining something that is not there. However, the question is not about interpreting this act as hallucination or pathology. Rather the importance lies in the fact that even at infancy, the human mind already has the capacity to be impacted by an object that is not present in flesh but is present as an idea. In other words, the physical absence or presence of the object can impact the subject the same way. The idea of the object can have similar impact on the human subject just as it would if it was the actual object present physically. Hence, the proposal within the context of perinatal counselling is that the idea of the baby may have the same or more impact on the person as the actual baby. Thus, it is proposed that the field of perinatal counselling extends its starting point to include the period before conception and extends well after the birth irrespective of whether there is a live birth or a stillbirth.

Furthermore, from engaging in practice-based research and decades of clinical experience of working within the areas of domestic violence, trauma and perinatal mental health it seems that within the context of counselling and psychotherapy, it is clinically beneficial to our clients to rethink the duration and timing of the perinatal period. The effect of the idea of the child may impact the person just as much or more or less than the actual child. Hence expanding the perinatal period's starting point to a time before conception is clinically beneficial to clients when it comes to therapy. Also it is much more realistic to expand the end point of perinatal period even further beyond one year. Why? It is reflected in some of the major learnings from the practice-based research that this model is based on. The clinical experience referred to here reflects on my clinical work with the following client groups:

- Working with young families with mild-to-moderate mental health emotional and behavioural difficulties in parent-child relationship
- Parent-parent relationship
- Family dynamics
- Couples' relationship post birth
- Young parents seeking parenting advice or support
- Retrospective account of patients recalling their childhood and their experience of parental mental health and emotional health in all other therapeutic contexts
- Clinical work with individuals and couples on sex and intimacy
- Trauma rehabilitation work with victims of trauma and torture including international protection seekers, war victims
- Specialised domestic violence clinical work which included decades of working with perpetrators of domestic violence

Clinical experience from the above major areas indicate that there is one thing in common: **a general expectation and/or occurrence of psychological/emotional/behavioural turmoil in the family dynamics, in one's sense of self, and in parent-child or couple relationships within the first five years of the birth of a child.** For instance, Men Overcoming Violent Emotion (MOVE Ireland), an organisation dedicated to working with perpetrators of domestic violence, reports both in their 2019 and 2020 audits that the majority age group of their men fall into the category 30–39 years old and the majority age group of the children of these men attending MOVE Ireland are between 0 and 5 years old (MOVE Ireland, 2023). In addition, research within the area of intimate partner violence (IPV) in pregnancy reports a shocking prevalence rate of any type of IPV in pregnancy ranging from 1.8% to 99.5% worldwide (Román-Gálvez et al., 2021). The WHO declared that between one in three and one in four women experience IPV (WHO, 2021) and the prevalence of IPV worldwide towards the mother of children under five varies from 22.8% (Buffarini et al, 2021) to 60.2% (Chilanga et al. 2020). This would indicate that IPV is still a gender issue and considering that female-bodied persons get pregnant, there is a huge overlap between IPV and the pregnancy/post birth period. This in turn means that there is an ethical duty towards perinatal clients. As counsellors and psychotherapists, one needs to be aware of the risks involved in this period, especially when a family has children under five. Thus, it is clinically necessary to extend the perinatal period beyond the medical model's guidelines to five years post birth.

From the above discussion, it is proposed that the following is the field of perinatal counselling. When working therapeutically, the perinatal period is to be conceptualised as extending from before conception to five years post birth with or without a baby. The perinatal counselling field is to include the following major topics: infertility, pregnancy loss, artificial reproductive technology (ART), prenatal, crisis pregnancy, abortion, grief and bereavement. Moreover, this field must include the complex intersections between perinatal mental health and gender, sexual orientation, sexual violence, domestic violence and abuse (DVA), IPV, ethnic identity, self-identity, role/purpose, parenting style, adverse childhood experiences (ACE) and trauma to name few.

Who is a perinatal client?

To identify who is a perinatal client, we need to question, "who is a mother". Similarly, we need to question "who is a father". At a surface level, these questions seem simple. But simple does not always mean easy. Attempting to answer these questions has stopped every single one of my Doctoral research participants all of whom were highly trained midwives with at least 15 years of clinical experience on average. "What/Who is a mother?", and "What/Who is a father?" – have yielded a variety of responses from participants of every workshop I conducted with health and allied health professionals such as nurses, midwives, medical practitioners, therapists, psychologists, social workers and others. One can outline certain qualities that a mother or father have or reminded them of or that they are meant to have or societally expected to have. They can also attempt to define a mother and a father by the birth of a baby. These are the types of responses that I received every time I asked these questions to my research participants and my audience at workshops and trainings. The problem is that even without possessing the qualities that are usually associated with the concept of a "mother", one can *feel or identify* as a mother. Similarly, even after giving birth to a healthy baby, one can struggle to *feel or identify* as a mother. While after a stillbirth one can continue to *feel or identify or believe* that they are a mother. Without a birth too, one can identify as a mother to a child that is biologically *not* theirs. One can even *feel or identify* as a mother to someone who has no apparent parent-child connection to them. So this is a significant question. Not an easy question as one would assume. It is far from simple to be able to identify as to who/what exactly *is* a mother. Similarly, Irish Perinatal Psychiatrist-Psychoanalyst Dr. Anthony McCarthy (2016) was grappled with this question too as he wrote,

> Is she a mother only if she has delivered a live baby? And kept it? But what if she had a miscarriage? Or if there was only an empty sac? Or if she had a termination? Or a stillbirth? … Each woman will respond personally and differently to the experience of being pregnant. For many it is a great joy, for others a shock they will adjust to, and for others it may be unwanted and she may or may not continue with the pregnancy… This "maternal impression" will be a key factor in how she thinks of or imagines what it is that is happening inside of her body and then how she reacts to this. Although this paper is titled: "who can call herself a mother?" it might equally be called: "When does an embryo or foetus become a baby for the woman and is it at that stage that she becomes a mother?

Hence, when it comes to identifying who is a perinatal client, it is more appropriate to be directed by one's clinical judgement and be guided by the possible presence or absence of the **question of becoming a mother or father**.

The scope of this model

As discussed above, this model operates within clinical settings where there is a question of "becoming a mother/father" involved in the person attending counselling, with or without a baby, during the period that starts much before conception and within five years post birth. Moreover, this model can be used with perinatal distress and other psychological difficulties during this period as long as they are not serious mental illness such as psychotic disorders. Within the field of perinatal mental health, the most relevant term is PND, also known as peripartum depression. This model can be used with clients displaying PND, but the best practice would be to follow one's own clinical judgment and/or work in conjunction with the local specialist perinatal mental health team.

Important to note here is that even though Jean-Etienne Esquirol was one of the first physicians in the mid-19th century to report cases of postpartum psychiatric illnesses, it was not until the 1990s that the DSM (APA, 1994) included a separate category of disorder for the psychological disturbances experienced by a woman in the perinatal period. In 1994, for the first time, MDD with postpartum onset was published in the DSM-IV (Segre & Davis, 2014). The DSM-5 (APA, 2017) has recently included a peripartum onset and thus the diagnosis of MDD) with peripartum onset is now added. Note that the phrasing is different in the DSM "MDD with peripartum onset" than the colloquially known term, "postnatal depression". So how did the general population know about this condition? Arguably it is celebrities like Brooke Shields in 2005 followed by "a host of other celebrities, bloggers, researchers and political advocates" that made PPD or PND "a household term" (Sparks, 2013). Note that the DSM did not have the umbrella terms PND and "baby blues", colloquially referred to the phenomena of woman's sufferings after childbirth, but they *are* included in lay vocabulary by the general public. This fact indicates something vital. Much before the clinicians identified these sufferings, the lay population knew what it is. Because from the dawn of civilisations, it seems people have been at some level familiar with the fact that something *can* happen during childbirth causing significant disturbance even where there has not been a death or unhealthy delivery. It seems that the general population have felt even before the clinicians named it, that there can be an overwhelming experience of a loss of "something" experienced by the mother, even when mother and baby are deemed healthy. **The experience of "becoming a mother" involves an experience of loss**. A sense of loss that can be multifaceted. Hence, whether there is an actual diagnosis or not, this model is operable in any perinatal situation where a sense of loss is experienced by the client in any shape and form. This can be situations such as unsuccessful conception, pregnancy loss, miscarriage, stillbirth, child loss and any other situation where the person feels a sense of loss and emptiness during the perinatal period.

Furthermore, there are three major considerations for clinicians to take into account when identifying the scope of this model.

1 The dominant paradigm that the clinicians are operating from. For example, do they prefer to use language such as disorder or difficulties or conditions or sufferings or similar to describe their patient's or client's account? Depending on their preferred language, clinicians must make clinical judgment as to whether it is appropriate to use this model with their patients or clients.
2 This model is designed to best work with situations ranging from mild sufferings to moderate non-psychotic psychiatric disorders. This model is not suitable for severe non-psychotic and any psychotic psychiatric disorders.
3 The model is usually applicable to cases that fall within the extended perinatal period proposed here. However, this model can be applied to cases where retrospective accounts are explored in therapy and the question of becoming a mother or father or the idea of a child is relevant in the recalling.

Conclusion

This chapter provided contextual background of the topic and its prevalence, defined some major terminologies relevant to this topic including the phrases "perinatal period" and "perinatal counselling", outlined how to determine if someone is a perinatal client for counselling purposes and finally defined the scope of the Becoming model. The next chapter will lay out the major theories and research that have helped shape this model which is arguably the only perinatal counselling model known to the author at the time of drafting this book and the major distinctive features of this model.

References

APA. (1994). *Diagnostic and statistical manual of mental disorders.* American Psychiatric Association.
APA. (2017). *Diagnostic and statistical manual of mental disorders: DSM-5.* American Psychiatric Association.
APA. (2023). APA Dictionary of Psychology. Retrieved from https://dictionary.apa.org/
Austin, M. P., Priest, S. R., & Sullivan, E. A. (2008). *Antenatal psychosocial assessment for reducing perinatal mental health morbidity. The Cochrane database of systematic reviews,* (4), CD005124. *https://doi.org/10.1002/14651858.CD005124.pub2*
Australian Institute of Health and Welfare. (2005). *Perinatal period.* Retrieved from http://meteor.aihw.gov.au/content/index.phtml/itemId/327314
Baldoni, F., & Giannotti, M. (2020). Perinatal distress in fathers: Toward a gender-based screening of paternal perinatal depressive and affective disorders. *Frontiers in Psychology, 11,* 1892. https://doi.org/10.3389/fpsyg.2020.01892

Buffarini, R., Coll, C. V. N., Moffitt, T., Freias da Silveira, M., Barros, F., & Murray, J. (2021). Intimate partner violence against women and child maltreatment in a Brazilian birth cohort study: co-occurrence and shared risk factors. *BMJ Global Health*, *6*(4), e004306. https://doi.org/10.1136/bmjgh-2020-004306

Button, S., Thornton, A., Lee, S., Shakespeare, J., & Ayers, S. (2017). Seeking help for perinatal psychological distress: A meta-synthesis of women's experiences. *British Journal of General Practice*, *67*(663). https://doi.org/10.3399/bjgp17x692549

Chilanga, E., Collin-Vezina, D., Khan, M. N., & Riley, L. (2020). Prevalence and determinants of intimate partner violence against mothers of children under-five years in Central Malawi. *BMC public health*, *20*(1), 1848. https://doi.org/10.1186/s12889-020-09910-z

HSE. (2017). Retrieved from https://www.hse.ie/eng/services/list/4/mental-health-services/specialist-perinatal-mental-health/specialist-perinatal-mental-health-services-model-of-care-2017.pdf

HSE. (2023a). Baby blues. Retrieved from https://www2.hse.ie/babies-children/parenting-advice/health-mental-wellbeing/baby-blues/

HSE. (2023b). *Specialist perinatal mental health: Health services executive*. Retrieved April 7, 2023, from https://www.hse.ie/eng/services/list/4/mental-health-services/specialist-perinatal-mental-health/

IFCA. (2022). Retrieved from https://fertilitycounsellors.ie/fertility-counselling/

Johnson, M., Schmeid, V., Lupton, S. J., Austin, M., Matthey, S. M., Kemp, L., & Yeo, A. E. (2012). Measuring perinatal mental health risk. *Archives of Women's Mental Health*, *15*(5), 375–386. https://doi.org/10.1007/s00737-012-0297-8

McCarthy, A. (2016). 'Who can call herself a mother?' *Psychotherapy and Counselling Journal of Australia*, *4*(1). http://pacja.org.au/?p=3002

McGrandles, A., & Duffy, T. (2012). Anxiety. In C. R. Martin (Ed.), *Perinatal mental health: A clinical guide* (pp. 25–42). M&K Publishing.

MOVE Ireland. (2023). *Annual report – move Ireland – move*. Retrieved April 7, 2023, from https://www.moveireland.ie/wp-content/uploads/2020/05/MOVE-Ireland-Annual-Report-2019-.pdf

NHS. (2019). Perinatal mental health services. Retrieved from https://www.longtermplan.nhs.uk/publication/perinatal/

RCPsych. (2018). Planning a pregnancy: Royal College of Psychiatrists. Retrieved from https://www.rcpsych.ac.uk/mental-health/treatments-and-wellbeing/planning-a-pregnancy

RCPsych. (2021). Retrieved from https://www.rcpsych.ac.uk/docs/default-source/improving-care/better-mh-policy/college-reports/college-report-cr232---perinatal-mental-heath-services.pdf?Status=Master&sfvrsn=82b10d7e_4

Román-Gálvez, R. M., Martín-Peláez, S., Fernández-Félix, B. M., Zamora, J., Khan, K. S., & Bueno-Cavanillas, A. (2021). Worldwide prevalence of intimate partner violence in pregnancy. A systematic review and meta-analysis. *Frontiers in Public Health*, *9*, 738459. https://doi.org/10.3389/fpubh.2021.738459

Scarff, J. R. (2019). Postpartum depression in men. *Innovations in Clinical Neuroscience*, *16*(5–6), 11–14.

Segre, L., & Davis, W. (2014) '*Postpartum depression and perinatal mood disorders in the DSM*'. www.postpartum.net. Retrieved April 29, 2020, from https://www.postpartum.net/wp-content/uploads/2014/11/DSM-5-Summary-PSI.pdf

Sparks, R. (2013). Sadness and Support: A Short History of Postpartum Depression. Accessed from https://medicine.uiowa.edu/bioethics/sites/medicine.uiowa.edu.bioethics/files/wysiwyg_uploads/2013%20Rysavy%20essay.pdf

Sultana, M. (2021). *Becoming a mother: A study of current and potential response to perinatal mental health* [Doctoral Thesis, UCD School of Medicine]. Retrieved April 4, 2023, from https://researchrepository.ucd.ie/bitstreams/42e5d42b-bba3-408f-acf2-283c48534da3/download

WHO. (2016). *Maternal and perinatal health*. Word Health Organisation. Retrieved from https://www.who.int/europe/health-topics/maternal-health#tab=tab_1

WHO. (2021). Retrieved from https://www.who.int/news/item/09-03-2021-devastatingly-pervasive-1-in-3-women-globally-experience-violence

WHO. (2022). *Mental health*. Word Health Organisation. Retrieved April 8, 2023, from https://www.who.int/news-room/fact-sheets/detail/mental-health-strengthening-our-response

Chapter 2

Distinct Features of Integration

Introduction

This chapter is aimed at providing two of the key information about the model that will assist the therapist in recognising pathways that they can integrate this model into their existing practice. This will be done by outlining (1) the three major reasons behind selecting the name of this model – "Becoming", indicating an ongoing process and (2) the five distinctive processes.

Three dynamic processes

There are a number of reasons that influenced the selection of the name of this model. Three of those reasons are captured here. (1) The name "Becoming" is meant to highlight that the subjective positions such as "mother" or "father" or "parent" are not boxes that one slip into after a birth. Rather, taking up these positions is a unique process. "Becoming" a mother/father/parent is an ongoing process as opposed to something that happens over night. This model also does not assume that one becomes a parent right after a birth. "Becoming" a mother/father/parent is a phenomenon that is independent of the presence or absence of an actual baby or a live or stillbirth. A phenomenon that is independent of any milestone, rather it is an ongoing journey. Hence, a person can be on the journey of "becoming" a parent much before and beyond the birth. (2) "Becoming" also refers to the dynamic process that continues to take place in their inner world, external world and inter-personal world as they transition to parenthood. The following chapters would demonstrate that becoming a mother/father/parent involves a restructuring of the subject's inner world, their psyche and their desire in a way that is unique and anything but static. Finally, (3) the name "Becoming" indicates the evolving process of application and integration of this model. The application of this model will be different based on the uniqueness of the client's history and current context. The integration of this model to one's existing ways of practising clinically will depend on the therapist's style and preference. Hence, the combination of several unique factors such as these make the application and integration of the Becoming model anything but constant.

DOI: 10.4324/9781003309710-3

The model has the potential to develop and grow with each application within the clinical setting.

Five distinctive features

There are several ways of achieving integration within the field of counselling and psychotherapy (Norcross & Goldfried, 2019). It is beyond the scope of this model to define some of the major categories such as theoretical integration, technical integration or technical eclecticism, common factors approach, assimilative integration, pluralism and so on. It is up to the therapist using this model to determine as to what category of integration this model can be labelled as. The next chapter will outline the major theoretical models and research findings that this model has borrowed from and integrated. This chapter will highlight the distinct features of this model that will help the therapist determine the type of integration that is at the heart of this model. The five distinctive features of this model that make it unique and "integrative" are below:

1 The Becoming model is possibly the only model within the perinatal mental health field that synthesises major theories and research into one single framework as a roadmap for the therapist.
2 The Becoming model focuses on the transition of the person unlike any other psychological model.
3 The Becoming model prioritises the impact of the foetus and/or the child on the mother and not the other way around.
4 The Becoming model has the potential to be used even before conception.
5 The Becoming model can be used by any qualified therapist irrespective of the theoretical school they align with.

1 The Becoming model is possibly the only model within the perinatal mental health field that synthesises major theories and research into one single framework as a roadmap for the therapist. There are several psychological theories that have the potential to understand and explain different elements of the transition that one goes through as they become a mother. For instance, the major theories that a therapist can draw from to conceptualise a person's sufferings and difficulties within this period are: Freudian psychoanalysis, Lacanian theories, Beck and Pavlovian cognitive and behavioural theories, Gestalt theories, humanistic theories, existential theories and on. This model is informed by these theories but does not require the therapist to be changing their own preferred theoretical framework or training background because this is a skeletal framework. A road map that has theoretical integration at its heart but can also be used atheoretically. A map that will allow the therapist to perform technical eclecticism. Furthermore, there are several theories on the development of Postnatal Depression (PND) or Postpartum Depression

(PPD) that informed this model, which are based on major research findings and outlined below:

a Biological theories

    i Withdrawal there (Galea et al., 2001; Schiller et al. 2014; Stoffel & Craft, 2004; Suda et al., 2008)

    ii Hypothalamic-pituitary-adrenal (HPA) axis theory (Dickens & Pawluski, 2018)

    iii Overall hormonal changes (Stewart et al., 2004)

b Obstetric theories

    i Obstetric complication theories (Blom et al., 2010; Koutra et al., 2016; Nielsen et al. 2005)

    ii Caesarean section theories (Boyce & Todd, 1992; Hannah et al., 1992; Nielsen et al. 2000)

    iii Unplanned/unwanted pregnancy (Beck, 1996, 2001; Finer & Zolna, 2016; Warner et al., 1996)

    iv Breastfeeding related theories (Dennis & McQueen, 2009; Hahn-Holbrook et al., 2013; Taveras et al., 2003)

c Clinical risk factors (Stewart et al., 2003)

    i History of depression

    ii Family history of depression

    iii Mood during pregnancy

    iv Prenatal anxiety

d Psychosocial theories (Stewart et al., 2003)

    i Psychodynamic theories

    ii Cognitive psychological theories

    iii Social interpersonal theories

    iv Behavioural theories

    v Evolutionary theories

e Social theories (Stewart et al., 2003)

    i Episodic events such as life events, catastrophic events and daily hassles

    ii Chronic stressors such as parenting stress, perceived stress, chronic strain, partner relationship quality and adult attachment style

As evident from the above list, there are several theories that capture aspects of the perinatal period from diverse disciplines. However, there is no framework that amalgamates these theories and provides a structure that can be used as a guide to navigate counselling sessions by therapists when working with perinatal patients. The "Becoming model" is thus a clinical framework for clinicians that integrates major existing theories and research from the field of perinatal mental health.

2   The Becoming model focuses on the transition of the person unlike any other psychological model. Most counselling theories relevant to the perinatal field are based on parent-child relationship such as family system theory and attachment theory to name few. They do not focus much on the person becoming a parent such as the intra-personal factor. Some theories do focus on the parent-parent relationship such as the inter-personal factor, but the emphasis may not remain on the transition of the person becoming a mother or a father. Some theories may also focus on the person's relationship to others such as the social world and the wider circle around them. However, the focus may not be on the person's transition of becoming a parent and navigating the wider circle and society. Especially, the existing research literature in this field does not yield much results that focus on the identity shift occurring within the person as they transition to becoming a mother/father. This integrative model bridges this gap by solely focusing on the person, their transition and their navigation of different aspects of life as they go through the perinatal period.

3   The Becoming model prioritises the impact of the foetus and/or the child on the mother and not the other way around. Most counselling theories relevant to the perinatal field mainly focus on the impact of the mother's or the father's or the parent's choices and behaviour on the child. For instance, perinatal psychology is a field that mainly investigates antenatal and postnatal development of the child and how it may be impacted by the mother's behaviour and choices. The Becoming model is developed based on the rationale that it is essential to address parental mental health in order to facilitate offspring's well-being. But this model focuses on just the opposite. Precisely because there are ample amount of literature, research and theories that examine offspring's health outcome impacted by parental mental health, choices and behaviour, but little attention has been paid the other way around. Current and existing literature does not seem to focus much on this reverse impact. This is why the Becoming model focuses on the impact that the baby has on the person who is becoming a mother/father/parent.

4   The Becoming model has the potential to be used even before conception. Extending from the previous point, the Becoming model also investigates the impact of the "idea of a baby" may have on the person becoming a parent. Hence, the person does not even have to have an actual baby in their life for this model to be used in clinical setting. When it comes to the human psyche, the Becoming model acknowledges that the idea of the baby is just as powerful as having the baby in reality. The Becoming model has the potential to be used even before conception. This is because in most cases, the "idea of a baby" occurs to the person much before the baby is conceived or born. The idea itself has the potential to impact the human psyche in the same way that an actual birth of a child would. Hence this integrative model is useful even during the period that a person is contemplating becoming a mother/father or actively trying to conceive or has experienced pregnancy loss or bereavement post birth.

5 The Becoming model can be used by any qualified therapist irrespective of the theoretical school they align to or are trained in or uses in a clinical setting. This integrative model is not a therapy itself. It is a clinical framework. Any qualified therapist trained in any school of counselling psychotherapy (e.g. psychoanalytic, cognitive-behavioural, humanistic, etc.) can use this framework to structure their sessions in terms of themes and sub-themes that they want to explore. Each of the themes and sub-themes of this model can be adapted and edited accordingly by the clinician to suit their own personality, preferred therapeutic style, theoretical orientation, clinical situation, therapeutic alliance and other factors that they see as relevant. This flexibility makes this model user-friendly and applicable to any therapeutic modality.

Conclusion

This chapter provided two of the key information about the model that will assist the therapist in recognising pathways that they can integrate this model into their existing practice. The next chapter will introduce the Becoming model, present the visual structure of the model along with outlining some of the major theories and basic assumptions that underpin this model.

References

Beck, C. T. (1996). A meta-analysis of predictors of postpartum depression. *Nursing Research, 45*(5), 297–303. https://doi.org/10.1097/00006199-199609000-00008

Beck, C. T. (2001). Predictors of postpartum depression: An update. *Nursing Research, 50*(5), 275–285. https://doi.org/10.1097/00006199-200109000-00004

Blom, E. A., Jansen, P. W., Verhulst, F. C., Hofman, A., Raat, H., Jaddoe, V. W., Coolman, M., Steegers, E. A., & Tiemeier, H. (2010). Perinatal complications increase the risk of postpartum depression. The generation R study. *BJOG: An International Journal of Obstetrics and Gynaecology, 117*(11), 1390–1398. https://doi.org/10.1111/j.1471-0528.2010.02660.x

Boyce, P. M., & Todd, A. L. (1992). Increased risk of postnatal depression after emergency caesarean section. *Medical Journal of Australia, 157*(3), 172–174. https://doi.org/10.5694/j.1326-5377.1992.tb137080.x

Dennis, C. L., & McQueen, K. (2009). The relationship between infant-feeding outcomes and postpartum depression: A qualitative systematic review. *Pediatrics, 123*(4), e736–e751. https://doi.org/10.1542/peds.2008-1629

Dickens, M. J., & Pawluski, J. L. (2018). The HPA axis during the perinatal period: Implications for perinatal depression. *Endocrinology, 159*(11), 3737–3746. https://doi.org/10.1210/en.2018-00677

Finer, L. B., & Zolna, M. R. (2016). Declines in unintended pregnancy in the United States, 2008–2011. *The New England Journal of Medicine, 374*(9), 843–852. https://doi.org/10.1056/NEJMsa1506575

Galea, L. A., Wide, J. K., & Barr, A. M. (2001). Estradiol alleviates depressive-like symptoms in a novel animal model of post-partum depression. *Behavioural Brain Research, 122*(1), 1–9. https://doi.org/10.1016/s0166-4328(01)00170-x

Hahn-Holbrook, J., Haselton, M. G., Dunkel Schetter, C., & Glynn, L. M. (2013). Does breastfeeding offer protection against maternal depressive symptomatology?: A prospective study from pregnancy to 2 years after birth. *Archives of Women's Mental Health, 16*(5), 411–422. https://doi.org/10.1007/s00737-013-0348-9

Hannah, M. E., Hannah, W. J., Hellmann, J., Hewson, S., Milner, R., & Willan, A. (1992). Induction of labor as compared with serial antenatal monitoring in post-term pregnancy. A randomized controlled trial. The Canadian multicenter post-term pregnancy trial group. *The New England Journal of Medicine, 326*(24), 1587–1592. https://doi.org/10.1056/NEJM199206113262402

Koutra, K., Simos, P., Triliva, S., Lionis, C., & Vgontzas, A. N. (2016). Linking family cohesion and flexibility with expressed emotion, family burden and psychological distress in caregivers of patients with psychosis: A path analytic model. *Psychiatry Research, 240*, 66–75, https://doi.org/10.1016/j.psychres.2016.04.017

Nielsen, P. E., Howard, B. C., Hill, C. C., Larson, P. L., Holland, R. H., & Smith, P. N. (2005). Comparison of elective induction of labor with favorable bishop scores versus expectant management: A randomized clinical trial. *The Journal of Maternal-Fetal & Neonatal Medicine, 18*(1), 59–64. https://doi.org/10.1080/14767050500139604

Nielsen, D., Videbech, P., Hedegaard, M., Dalby, J., & Secher, N. J. (2000). Postpartum depression: Identification of women at risk. *BJOG: An International Journal of Obstetrics and Gynaecology, 107*(10), 1210–1217. https://doi.org/10.1111/j.1471-0528.2000.tb11609.x

Norcross, J. C., & Goldfried, M. R. (2019). *Handbook of psychotherapy integration*. Oxford University Press.

Schiller, C. E., Meltzer-Brody, S., & Rubinow, D. R. (2014). The role of reproductive hormones in postpartum depression. *CNS Spectrums, 20*(1), 48–59. https://doi.org/10.1017/s1092852914000480

Stewart, D. E., Robertson, E., Dennis, C. L., & Grace, S. (2004). An evidence-based approach to post-partum depression. *World Psychiatry: Official Journal of the World Psychiatric Association (WPA), 3*(2), 97–98. Retrieved from https://poliklinika-harni.hr/images/uploads/380/who-postpartalna-depresija.pdf

Stoffel, E. C., & Craft, R. M. (2004). Ovarian hormone withdrawal-induced "depression" in female rats. *Physiology & Behavior, 83*(3), 505–513. https://doi.org/10.1016/j.physbeh.2004.08.033

Suda, S., Segi-Nishida, E., Newton, S. S., & Duman, R. S. (2008). A postpartum model in rat: Behavioral and gene expression changes induced by ovarian steroid deprivation. *Biological Psychiatry, 64*(4), 311–319. https://doi.org/10.1016/j.biopsych.2008.03.029

Taveras, E. M., Capra, A. M., Braveman, P. A., Jensvold, N. G., Escobar, G. J., & Lieu, T. A. (2003). Clinician support and psychosocial risk factors associated with breastfeeding discontinuation. *Pediatrics, 112*(1 Pt 1), 108–115. https://doi.org/10.1542/peds.112.1.108

Warner, R., Appleby, L., Whitton, A., & Faragher, B. (1996). Demographic and obstetric risk factors for postnatal psychiatric morbidity. *The British Journal of Psychiatry: The Journal of Mental Science, 168*(5), 607–611. https://doi.org/10.1192/bjp.168.5.607

Chapter 3

Becoming Model

Introduction

The previous chapter described the rationale behind the naming process of this model and the distinctive features of this model. This chapter will introduce the Becoming model itself by providing a visual representation of it. The chapter will then outline some of the major theories that have been integrated to design this model. Next, the chapter will outline the themes and sub-themes of this model. Finally, some of the basic assumptions underpinning this model will be laid out for the readers.

Providing pathways

The Becoming model provides the therapist with possible pathways to explore during sessions. This is a road map rather that the therapist can use should they wish to seek direction in their sessions as their clients transition to parenthood. The transition to parenthood is a process that is ongoing. It does not usually happen overnight for all. Yet the general expectation seems to be that as soon as the child is handed over from the womb to the birthing person or to their significant other, the person is meant to "become" a mom/dad/parent. Many of us do not slip into these neatly tied categories overnight just like that! This model is designed to incorporate everyone going through the perinatal period despite how smooth or rough their transition *is* into parenthood. Transition is a key term in relation to this model. Because at a foundational level this model assumes parenthood is anything but a destination. One does not reach "it", but rather it is something one works towards and transitions to it. The journey they take on the way to "parenthood" is more important than the destination. Furthermore, "parenthood" is a concept that is socially constructed, highly value-laden and literally everyone has a different definition of this term. Parenthood is a state of mind. Transitioning to parenthood is a journey of "becoming". This model captures most of the major and relevant pathways that one may travel or stumble across on that journey.

Underpinning theories and research

The Becoming Model is a constellation of practice-based research and research-based practice. This is an amalgamation of several major classical and contemporary

DOI: 10.4324/9781003309710-4

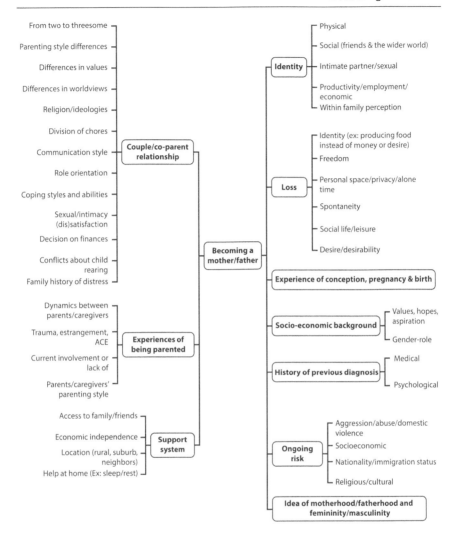

Figure 3.1 The Becoming model (Intellectual Property Office of Ireland, 2021).

Source: Author

psychological theories, research results from major projects across the globe both past and current, the author's own clinical experience and author's own research projects. Following is a brief list of major theories and research that composed

- Sigmund Freud's psychoanalytic theories such as the Drive theory, Femininity (Freud et al., 2001a, 2001b, 2001c, 2001d, 2001e, 2001f, 2001g, 2001h, 2001i, 2001j, 2001k, 2001l, 2001m, 2001n, 2001o, 2001p, 2001q, 2001r, 2001s, 2001t, 2001u, 2001v, 2001w, 2001x)
- Jacques Lacan's major psychoanalytic concepts such as object petit a, mirror stage (Lacan, 1977, 1988a, 1988b, 1992, 1993, 1998, 2006, 2007, 2014, 2015, 2016, 2018, 2019, 2020; Lacan et al., 2006)

- Murray Bowen's (1976, 1978) family theories concepts such as differentiation of self-scale, triangles, cutoff, family projection process, multigenerational transmission process, sibling position and emotional processes of society.
- Tajfel and Turner's (1986) Social identity theory
- Sociological theory on Intersectionality (Crenshaw, 1991)
- Sociological theory of Pierre Bourdieu's Habitus, Capital and Field theory (Bourdieu, 1980, 1984, 1986)
- Sociological theory of Michel Foucault's Power and Knowledge (Foucault, 1991, 1998; Foucault & Gordon, 2015);
- Neuroscience findings on the structural changes in brain during the perinatal period
- The bio-psychosocial model (Engel, 1978, 1980)
- Bronfenbrenner ecological systems model (Bronfenbrenner, 1992)
- Theoretical framework developed using Freudian and Lacanian theories for clinical application in the field of human psychosexuality (Sultana, 2018)
- Theoretical framework developed to conceptualise perinatal mental health difficulties informed by classical and contemporary theories and Doctoral research on midwives' experiences of working with perinatal mental health difficulties (Sultana, 2021)

Breakdown of the themes

This model consists of ten major themes and 40 sub-themes. Each chapter is dedicated to a major theme. The chapters will guide the reader by providing some basic foundational knowledge of the theme such as some working definitions relevant to the theme and/or snippets of the latest meta-analytic research situating the importance of the theme. It is up to the therapist as to how they decide to explore these topics with their clients. The definitions and research presented on each themes and sub-themes are meant to be comprehensive and/or directive. Rather they can be seen as a conversation starter with clients or a general point to start from if the therapist is seeking such guidance. This book does not aim to provide clinical techniques of exploring these topics. Rather the model aims to highlight the relevance of the themes, rational for including them as part of the model and their connection to perinatal mental health. This model also does not provide any particular theoretical explanations. Hence, the therapist has the flexibility to use their preferred clinical techniques and theoretical conceptualisation for each of these themes. However, not every theme will be relevant to every client. The therapist must be guided by their own theoretical background, training style, clinical judgment and relevance in exploring any of these themes.

- Theme 1: Identity (see Chapter 4)

  a Physical
  b Social (friends and the wider world)

c   Intimate partner/sexual
d   Productivity/employment/economic
e   Within family perception

- Theme 2: Idea of motherhood/fatherhood femininity/masculinity (see Chapter 5)
- Theme 3: Loss (Symbolic) (see Chapter 6)

a   Identity
b   Freedom
c   Personal space/privacy/alone time
d   Spontaneity
e   Social life/leisure
f   Desire/desirability

- Theme 4: Experience of conception, pregnancy and birth (see Chapter 7)
- Theme 5: Couple and/or co-parent relationship (see Chapter 8)

a   From two to threesome
b   Parenting style differences
c   Differences in values
d   Differences in world-views
e   Perspectives on religion/ideals/ideologies
f   Perspectives on division of chores
g   Communication style
h   Role orientation
i   Coping styles and abilities
j   Sexual/intimacy (dis)satisfaction
k   Decision on finances
l   Conflicts about child rearing
m   Family history of distress (including trauma)

- Theme 6: Experiences of being parented (see Chapter 9)

a   Dynamics between parents/caregivers
b   Trauma, estrangement, Adverse Childhood Experience (ACE)
c   Current involvement or lack of
d   Parents/caregivers' parenting style

- Theme 7: Socio-economic background (see Chapter 10)

a   Values, hopes, aspiration
b   Gender-roles

- Theme 8: History of previous diagnosis (see Chapter 11)

a   Medical
b   Psychological

- Theme 9: Ongoing risk (see Chapter 12)

    a Aggression/abuse/coercive control/domestic violence
    b Risks particular to socio-economic group
    c Nationality/immigration status
    d Religious/cultural

- Theme 10: Support system (see Chapter 13)

    a Access to family/friends
    b Economic independence
    c Location (rural, suburb, neighbours)
    d Help at home (e.g. sleep/rest)

Underpinning assumptions and presuppositions

Guilt everywhere

One of the most common themes that keep coming up when working therapeutically with perinatal clients is Guilt. This model does not particularly have a theme dedicated to this topic because each and every theme and sub-themes in this model have the potential to uncover a sense of guilt associated to them with the client during their perinatal period. For example, the person may be guilty because they believe they returned to work too quickly after the birth; they may feel guilty for wanting to return to work; guilty for not being there for their children enough; guilty for being annoyed and upset with their children and partner; guilty for not being patient enough; guilty for not being appreciative enough of having healthy children while others around them are not so "lucky" to conceive or to have a family at all; guilty for resenting their partners who seemingly can enjoy more sleep, leisure time and have adult conversation with colleagues; guilty for not being able to manage work and home like other mothers; guilty for not being content and happy and so on… It is assumed that when working with this model, it is up to the therapist as to how they will address latent and manifest content related to guilt. The model is designed with the theme of guilt in mind as a potential area to be explored as part of all the themes and sub-themes. Hence, there are no separate themes of guilt in this model as the assumption is that it can be everywhere!

We all assume

As human beings we all have some presuppositions and assumptions in our minds. It is essential for the smooth functioning of society that one assumes and have presuppositions. For instance, if someone has been invited to a party and they have confirmed they are coming, it is assumed that they are coming unless they say otherwise. However, therapists are trained *not to* assume. Therapists know that the human mind can function mysteriously, our decisions can sometimes make no sense and behaviour can defy all logic. Therapists are trained to be aware of their own presuppositions and assumptions. Yet, there are some blind spots among all therapists. Just as there are blind spots in all humans. Despite their best efforts to be aware of their own biases or presuppositions, therapists may have certain expectations or automatic beliefs about the perinatal period just as lay people may have about this field. Some of the basic assumptions that most lay people and most professionals working both within and outside this area may have about the perinatal period are outlined below.

Perfection

We live in a world where "perfection" is encouraged and rewarded even when it comes at the cost of one's health and mental health. There is an overall expectation that women can manage both home and work "perfectly". This expectation of a "constant balancing act" has emerged in our society over time for a number of reasons that are beyond the scope of this book to capture. However, one such reason behind this intensification of such expectation in recent times is social media. This mythical mother who manages to balance everything perfectly is a construction of the social discourse where the very foundation is nothing but filtered truth. In other words, social media has created unrealistic expectations among mothers based on the production and circulation of fake and untrue material. Minding a child is a full-time job. Expecting to have a full-time job of minding the child at home and in addition having formal employment(s) outside home is not something that is realistic or reasonable or achievable or sustainable for all. The becoming model assumes that there is no woman in this world that can manage all of the aspects of their life, especially in their perinatal period and manages that perfectly!

Times of turmoil

This model also assumes that the perinatal period is a problematic period. It is up to the perinatal clients and their significant others as to how they would navigate this period and maintain peace and respect for all involved. Some do it without professional support, and some may need professional support in navigating these times. This assumption that the perinatal period is a time of upheaval is in direct contradiction to the capitalist society's portrayal of the perinatal period. We live in a society where Hollywood and social media sell a picture that does not reflect reality for most people. Consider the dream picture of a seemingly happy and content-looking woman sitting in her rocking chair in her suburban house comforting a baby. Perhaps being kissed on the cheek by a loving partner. A picture that often comes to mind for most of us (both therapists and lay) as we associate this to the concepts of "pregnancy" and "becoming a mother" after years of being bombarded by the media. This is also similar to the mental picture of an "instagram-mom" who does palates in the morning, swims in the afternoon, manages to get her PowerPoint presentation done for the office and presents it to the board somewhere in between palate and lunch and also manages to put a healthy plate of home cooked food for everyone at the table at night! These associations and exceptions are fuelled by hours of scrolling on our phone on social media. Similarly, the advertisements of baby products are far from reality. They always display babies as clean tiny humans who are smiling or sleeping peacefully. Their mothers and/or fathers seem happy wearing clean clothes with no spit or baby puke on them. They have freshly washed hair that is perfectly styled. They also manage to have time to wear some minimal makeup. While these pictures may resemble reality for some, for the vast majority of humans on this planet these are just the opposite of their reality. Moreover, giving birth itself may trigger psychosis for a small portion of the population, let alone the statistical reality that teaches us about the high prevalence of perinatal distress, baby blues, postnatal depression and the onset and relapse of other mental health difficulties including serious mental illness in the perinatal period. Hence, the Becoming model assumes that the perinatal period is anything but safe or peaceful. It is a time of turmoil like no other. It has the potential to evoke anxiety like no other. It has ripple effects that can impact all and/or several aspects of one's life. It can also be navigated by support, mutual respect and love.

Primacy of the uniqueness within us

Most professionals and lay persons tend to believe that pregnancy, birth and child-rearing are natural phenomena. Some of us believe that something kicks in within the woman automatically as they become a mother. Hence at some level, the assumption is that becoming a mother/father/parent is familiar, in-built and natural. While that may be the case for some, it is also NOT the case for many. In believing this theory of nature, inbuilt instinct and familiarity, we assume that becoming a mother/father/parent is at some level similar for everyone. However, this journey is anything but similar. Individual differences play a huge role within this field. One becomes surprised by even their own reactions and responses to the stressors during this period. Our uniqueness comes to the foreground like never before during this period. This model assumes that each and every human being is as individual and unique as their fingerprints. No matter how similar two people may seem, no one and absolutely no one in this world has the same fingerprints as you! Even identical twins do not share the same fingerprints. The current population of the planet is about eight billion in 2023 according to the Live Worldometer website (Worldometers, 2023). That means there are about eight billion individuals with eight billion patterns of fingerprints that are unique. That is not even counting those humans that lived on this planet before us, since the time of the Dinosaurs or Adam, whichever theory on the dawn of civilisation one believes in. In essence, it is impossible for any human to capture all the eight billion and more patterns of individuality that existed, exist and will continue to emerge and disappear from this planet. But the human mind tends to search for patterns, create categories, then puts them together based on similarities and dissimilarities and labels them assuming everything under a label is similar to one another. In reality, no two human beings are the same, especially not while they are going through the perinatal period. Even though they may have been given a label to indicate similarities. Hence, no research, no dataset, no psychological model, no matter how comprehensive they are, nothing will ever be able to capture a person's individuality in its entirety. The Becoming model does not claim to do so either. Simply because every human is different and unique in their own way, no matter how similar they or their stories may seem on the surface. Hence this model assumes that the themes and the sub-themes are a general roadmap for the therapist to travel along with their clients based on their own clinical judgement as every client's story and every therapeutic session are at some level unique. No matter how similar they may seem from the outside, the stories and sessions are unique just like one's fingerprints.

Conclusion

This chapter has introduced the Becoming model in its visual form. It has also outlined some of the major theories that have been integrated to design this model. The chapter then outlined the major themes and sub-themes of this model and highlighted some of the basic assumptions underpinning this model. The next chapter will explore the first major theme of this model: Identity.

References

Bourdieu, P. (1980). *The logic of practice*. Stanford University Press.

Bourdieu, P. (1984). *Distinction: A social critique of the judgement of taste*. Routledge.

Bourdieu, P. (1986). The forms of capital. In J. Richardson (Ed.), *Handbook of theory and research for the sociology of education*. Greenwood Press.

Bowen, M. (1976). Theory in the practice of psychotherapy. In P. J. Guerin (Ed.), *Family therapy*. Gardner.

Bowen, M. (1978). *Family therapy in clinical practice*. Aronson.

Bronfenbrenner, U. (1992). Ecological systems theory. In R. Vasta (Ed.), *Six theories of child development: Revised formulations and current issues* (pp. 187–249). Jessica Kingsley Publishers.

Crenshaw, K. (1991). Mapping the margins: Intersectionality, identity politics, and violence against women of color. *Stanford Law Review*, *43*(6), 1241. https://doi.org/10.2307/1229039

Engel, G. L. (1978). The need for a new medical model: A challenge for biomedicine. *Dimensions of Behavior*, 3–21. https://doi.org/10.1016/b978-0-409-95009-0.50006-1

Engel, G. L. (1980). The clinical application of the biopsychosocial model. *American Journal of Psychiatry*, *137*(5), 535–544. https://doi.org/10.1176/ajp.137.5.535

Foucault, M. (1991). *Discipline and punish: The birth of a prison*. Penguin.

Foucault, M. (1998). *The history of sexuality: The will to knowledge*. Penguin.

Foucault, M., & Gordon, C. (2015). *Power/knowledge: Selected interviews and other writings 1972–1977*. Vintage Books.

Freud, S., Strachey, J., Freud, A., Strachey, A., & Tyson, A. (2001a). *The standard edition of the complete psychological works of Sigmund Freud. Vol. I (1886–1899): Pre-psycho-analytic publications and unpublished drafts*. Vintage.

Freud, S., Strachey, J., Freud, A., Strachey, A., & Tyson, A. (2001b). *The standard edition of the complete psychological works of Sigmund Freud. Vol. II (1893–1895): Studies on hysteria*. Vintage.

Freud, S., Strachey, J., Freud, A., Strachey, A., & Tyson, A. (2001c). *The standard edition of the complete psychological works of Sigmund Freud. Vol. III (1893–1899): Early psycho-analytic publications*. Vintage.

Freud, S., Strachey, J., Freud, A., Strachey, A., & Tyson, A. (2001d). *The standard edition of the complete psychological works of Sigmund Freud. Vol. IV (1900): The interpretation of dreams (first part)*. Vintage.

Freud, S., Strachey, J., Freud, A., Strachey, A., & Tyson, A. (2001e). *The standard edition of the complete psychological works of Sigmund Freud. Vol. V (1900–1901): The interpretation of dreams (second part) and on dreams*. Vintage.

Freud, S., Strachey, J., Freud, A., Strachey, A., & Tyson, A. (2001f). *The standard edition of the complete psychological works of Sigmund Freud. Vol. VI (1901): The psychopathology of everyday life*. Vintage.

Freud, S., Strachey, J., Freud, A., Strachey, A., & Tyson, A. (2001g). *The standard edition of the complete psychological works of Sigmund Freud. Vol. VII (1901–1905): A case of hysteria, three essays on sexuality and other works*. Vintage.

Freud, S., Strachey, J., Freud, A., Strachey, A., & Tyson, A. (2001h). *The standard edition of the complete psychological works of Sigmund Freud. Vol. VIII (1905): Jokes and their relation to the unconscious*. Vintage.

Freud, S., Strachey, J., Freud, A., Strachey, A., & Tyson, A. (2001i). *The standard edition of the complete psychological works of Sigmund Freud. Vol. IX (1906–1908): Jensen's 'Gradiva' and other works*. Vintage.

Freud, S., Strachey, J., Freud, A., Strachey, A., & Tyson, A. (2001j). *The standard edition of the complete psychological works of Sigmund Freud. Vol. X (1909): Two case histories ('Little Hans' and the 'Rat Man')*. Vintage.

Freud, S., Strachey, J., Freud, A., Strachey, A., & Tyson, A. (2001k). *The standard edition of the complete psychological works of Sigmund Freud. Vol. XI (1910): Five lectures on psycho-analysis, Leonardo da Vinci and other works*. Vintage.

Freud, S., Strachey, J., Freud, A., Strachey, A., & Tyson, A. (2001l). *The standard edition of the complete psychological works of Sigmund Freud. Vol. XII (1911–1913): The case of Schreber, papers on technique and other works*. Vintage.

Freud, S., Strachey, J., Freud, A., Strachey, A., & Tyson, A. (2001m). *The standard edition of the complete psychological works of Sigmund Freud. Vol. XIII (1913–1914): Totem and taboo and other works*. Vintage.

Freud, S., Strachey, J., Freud, A., Strachey, A., & Tyson, A. (2001n). *The standard edition of the complete psychological works of Sigmund Freud. Vol. XIV (1914–1916): On the history of the psycho-analytic movement, papers on metapsychology and other works*. Vintage.

Freud, S., Strachey, J., Freud, A., Strachey, A., & Tyson, A. (2001o). *The standard edition of the complete psychological works of Sigmund Freud. Vol. XV (1915–1916): Introductory lectures on psycho-analysis (Parts I and II)*. Vintage.

Freud, S., Strachey, J., Freud, A., Strachey, A., & Tyson, A. (2001p). *The standard edition of the complete psychological works of Sigmund Freud. Vol. XVI (1916–1917): Introductory lectures on psycho-analysis (Part III): Introductory lectures on psycho-analysis (Parts I and II)*. Vintage.

Freud, S., Strachey, J., Freud, A., Strachey, A., & Tyson, A. (2001q). *The standard edition of the complete psychological works of Sigmund Freud. Vol. XVII (1917–1919): An infantile neurosis and other works.* London: Vintage.

Freud, S., Strachey, J., Freud, A., Strachey, A., & Tyson, A. (2001r). *The standard edition of the complete psychological works of Sigmund Freud. Vol. XVIII (1920–1922): Beyond the pleasure principle, group psychology and other works.* Vintage.

Freud, S., Strachey, J., Freud, A., Strachey, A., & Tyson, A. (2001s). *The standard edition of the complete psychological works of Sigmund Freud. Vol. XIX (1923–1925): The ego and the id and other works.* Vintage.

Freud, S., Strachey, J., Freud, A., Strachey, A., & Tyson, A. (2001t). *The standard edition of the complete psychological works of Sigmund Freud. Vol. XX (1925–1926): An autobiographical study, inhibitions, symptoms and anxiety, the question of lay analysis and other works.* Vintage.

Freud, S., Strachey, J., Freud, A., Strachey, A., & Tyson, A. (2001u). *The standard edition of the complete psychological works of Sigmund Freud. Vol. XXI (1927–1931): The future of an illusion, civilization and its discontents, and other works.* Vintage.

Freud, S., Strachey, J., Freud, A., Strachey, A., & Tyson, A. (2001v). *The standard edition of the complete psychological works of Sigmund Freud. Vol. XXII (1932–1936): New introductory lectures on psycho-analysis and other works.* Vintage.

Freud, S., Strachey, J., Freud, A., Strachey, A., & Tyson, A. (2001w). *The standard edition of the complete psychological works of Sigmund Freud. Vol. XXIII (1937–1939): Moses and monotheism, an outline of psycho-analysis and other works.* Vintage.

Freud, S., Strachey, J., Freud, A., Strachey, A., & Tyson, A. (2001x). *The standard edition of the complete psychological works of Sigmund Freud. Vol. XXIV: Indexes and bibliographies.* Vintage.

Intellectual Property Office of Ireland. (2021). Integrative Perinatal Counselling: The Becoming Model (Sultana 2021) : Register of Trademarks Journal No. 2453. Retrieved from https://eregister.ipoi.gov.ie/register/TMRegister.aspx?idappli=266106

Lacan, J. (1977). *Book XI: The four fundamental concepts of psychoanalysis, 1964* (J.-A. Miller, Ed. & A. Sheridan, Trans.). W.W. Norton and Company.

Lacan, J. (1988a). *Book I: Freud's papers on technique, 1953–1954* (J.-A. Miller, Ed. & J. Forrester, Trans.). W.W. Norton and Company.

Lacan, J. (1988b). *Book II: The ego in Freud's theory and in the technique of psychoanalysis, 1954–1955* (J.-A. Miller, Ed. & S. Tomaselli, Trans.). W.W. Norton and Company.

Lacan, J. (1992). *Book VII: The ethics of psychoanalysis, 1959–1960* (J.-A. Miller, Ed. & D. Porter, Trans.). W.W. Norton and Company.

Lacan, J. (1993). *Book III: The psychoses 1955–1956* (J.-A. Miller, Ed. & R. Grigg, Trans.). W.W. Norton and Company.

Lacan, J. (1998). *Book XX: Encore, 1972–1973* (J.-A. Miller, Ed. & B. Fink, Trans.). W.W. Norton and Company.

Lacan, J. (2006). *Book XXIII: The sinthome, 1975–1976* (J.-A. Miller, Ed. & A.R. Price, Trans.). Polity.

Lacan, J. (2007). *Book XVII: The other side of psychoanalysis, 1969–1970* (J.-A. Miller, Ed. & R. Grigg, Trans.). W.W. Norton and Company.

Lacan, J. (2014). *Book X: Anxiety, 1962–1963* (J.-A. Miller, Ed. & A.R. Price, Trans.). Polity.

Lacan, J. (2015). *Book XIII: Transference, 1961–1962* (J.-A. Miller, Ed. & B. Fink, Trans.). Polity.

Lacan, J. (2016). *Book V: Formations of the unconscious, 1957–1958* (J.-A. Miller, Ed. & R. Grigg, Trans.). Polity.

Lacan, J. (2018). *Book XIX: ... or worse, 1971–1972* (J.-A. Miller, Ed. & A.R. Price, Trans.). Polity.

Lacan, J. (2019). *Book VI: Desire and its interpretation, 1958–1959* (J.-A. Miller, Ed. & B. Fink, Trans.). Polity.

Lacan, J. (2020). *Book IV: The object relation, 1956–1957* (J.-A. Miller, Ed. & A.R. Price, Trans.). Polity.

Lacan, J., Fink, H., & Grigg, R. (Collaborators). (2006). *Écrits* (first complete edition in English) (B. Fink, Trans.). W. W. Norton & Company.

Sultana, M. (2018). *The castration complex: What is so natural about sexuality?* Routledge, Taylor & Francis Group.

Sultana, M. (2021). *Becoming a mother: A study of current and potential response to Perinatal Mental Health.* [Doctoral Thesis, UCD School of Medicine]. Retrieved April 4, 2023, from https://researchrepository.ucd.ie/bitstreams/42e5d42b-bba3-408f-acf2-283c48534da3/download

Tajfel, H., & Turner, J. C. (1986). The Social Identity Theory of Intergroup Behavior. In: Worchel, S. and Austin, W. G., Eds., Psychology of Intergroup Relation, Hall Publishers, Chicago, 7–24.

Tajfel, H., & Turner, J. C. (2004). The social identity theory of intergroup behavior. In J. T. Jost & J. Sidanius (Eds.), *Political psychology: Key readings* (pp. 276–293). Psychology Press. https://doi.org/10.4324/9780203505984-16

Worldometers. (2023). Retrieved from https://www.worldometers.info/

Chapter 4

Identity

Sub-themes:

a Physical identity
b Social (friends and the wider world)
c Intimate partner(s)/sexual
d Productivity/employment/economic
e Within family perception

Introduction

The central aim of this chapter is to provide an outline of some of the major theories on maternal identity during the perinatal period. The theme is identity is a small specialised clinical field that has remained less researched and documented than other topics within the area of perinatal mental health. Hence, the following sections will provide a bird's eye view of the two most notable theorists' and practitioners' accounts on this theme for the therapist's consideration. The chapter will then highlight the sub-themes. Finally, some the chapter will lay out some possible questioning styles that may help the therapist explore the client's perception of herself as she transitions to motherhood.

New identity ... transition

One of the ten major themes of this model is Identity. Enquiring maternal or paternal identity forma psychological perspective during the perinatal period is a very narrow field. Not much research and theories focus on this aspect. Especially when it comes to the impact a child or the idea of a child may have on one's identity, this has remained as a road less travelled. The following section will thus draw from the key figures within this narrow field and highlight the major contemporary theories that have emerged in recent times to conceptualise maternal or paternal identity as one transition to parenthood. For the purposes of this model, the term "Identity" is being used in the same sense as it is described in the American Psychological Association's (APA) Dictionary (APA, 2023).

> An individual's sense of self defined by (a) a set of physical, psychological, and interpersonal characteristics that is not wholly shared with any other person and (b) a range of affiliations (e.g., ethnicity) and social roles. Identity involves a sense of continuity, or the feeling that one is the same person today that one was yesterday or last year (despite physical or other changes). Such a sense is derived from one's body sensations; one's body image; and the feeling that one's memories, goals, values, expectations, and beliefs belong to the self. Also called **personal identity**.

DOI: 10.4324/9781003309710-5

The importance of exploring "Identity" within this field has been highlighted in classical psychoanalysis in the works of Sigmund Freud and later Jacques Lacan (Sultana, 2018, 2021). In recent times among contemporary theorists within this narrow field, Reproductive Psychiatry is the discipline that is worth drawing from. This is a branch of Medicine and most importantly, it is a title used by several psychiatrists in the USA to specialise and practice within the field of perinatal mental health. Within the Irish and UK context, Perinatal Psychiatry is the term often used to denote the same field. There are two legendary American practitioners whose work have been invaluable in illustrating the importance of exploring the topic of identity within this field. Dr. Alexandra Sacks, MD is one of those two reproductive psychiatrists. She is affiliated with the Women's Program at the Columbia University Medical Center. Her psychiatry is psychoanalytically informed by her training which she undertook at the Columbia University Center for Psychoanalytic Training. In 2017, Dr. Sacks published an article in the New York Times, "The Birth of a Mother", which became the number one most read article in the The New York Times Well Family section in 2017 (Sack, 2022). The article (Sacks, 2017) mainly centred around the topics presented in a book with a similar title *The Birth of a Mother: How the Experience of Motherhood Changes You Forever* written by Daniel Stern M.D. in 2001. Dr. Stern a psychiatrist at the University of Geneva is the other and primary significant contributor within this field. His seminal text *The Interpersonal World of the Infant* (Stern, [1985] 2001) is an excellent source of knowledge within this field focusing on the theme of Identity.

Both Sacks (2017) and Stern (2001) emphasised a phenomenon that has remained less explored (theoretically and clinically) and yet so seemingly familiar to the human race, i.e., the phenomena of "becoming a mother". They both focused on the woman's transition to motherhood and the changes that occur in her psychological landscape as she transitions to motherhood. The following are two significant quotes from these two reproductive psychiatrists highlighting the importance of identity as a major theme within this field.

…a mother has to be born psychologically just as her baby has to be born physically… There are many books about the physiological and practical aspects of motherhood, but far less is written about the mental world where the new identity is formed. Becoming a mother is accomplished by the labor each woman performs on the landscape of her mind… a deep and private realm of experience.

(Stern, 2001, p. 3)

The process of becoming a mother, which anthropologists call "matrescence," has been largely unexplored in the medical community. Instead of focusing on the woman's identity transition, more research is focused on how the baby turns out. But a woman's story, in addition to how her psychology impacts her parenting, is important to examine, too…understanding the psychology of pregnant and postpartum women can help promote healthier parenting. Mothers with greater awareness of their own psychology may be more empathetic to their children's emotions.

(Sacks, 2017)

Matrescence ... identity

The term *matrescence* is a concept coined by the medical anthropologist Dana Louise Raphael (1973) denoting a particular type of transition. To understand *matrescence,* one needs to ask if transition is a relevant term to describe the phenomena of "becoming a mother"? Is there even a term that exists that refers to the "developmental framework for the transition to motherhood" (Athan, 2023; Athan & Reel, 2015)? Dr. Athan is a scholar who aimed to respond to that question in the recent times. Athan (2016) "applies a feminist-informed, positive psychology and spiritual well-being framework in addition to traditional clinical and psychoanalytic lenses to her scholarship and women's narratives" with an aim to understand the transition to motherhood. During her clinical psychology training Dr. Aurelie Athan, a reproductive psychologist at the Columbia University, "was unable to find good explanatory models for the psychological transition to motherhood" despite "an extensive literature review of all of the scientific studies in the past 25 years, in a variety of disciplines, including psychology, psychiatry, medicine, nursing and others" (Athan, 2023). She then came across a medical anthropologist and a Columbia University graduate, reproductive psychologist Dana Louise Raphael's thesis (1926–2016).

Raphael (1975) coined the term *Matrescence* which is similar to the term Adolescence. Raphael believed that a similar transition is experienced by the woman as she becomes a mother to what a child experiences while transitioning to adolescence. According to her student Athan (2016), the following is a working definition of this term.

> ...developmental passage where a woman transitions through pre-conception, pregnancy and birth, surrogacy or adoption, to the postnatal period and beyond. The exact length of matrescence is individual, recurs with each child, and may arguably last a lifetime! The scope of the changes encompass multiple domains –bio-psycho-social-political-spiritual– and can be likened to the developmental push of adolescence. Increased attention to mothers has spurred new findings, from neuroscience to economics, and supports the rationale for a new field of study known as matrescence. Such an arena would allow the roundtable of specialists to come together and advance our understanding of this life passage.

Matrescence is a term that Athan (2016) through her teaching and talks promoted. Her promotion of the term is aimed at providing a "developmental model of motherhood to normalize the psychological transition women were experiencing", and later on the term appeared in The New York Times article The Birth of the Mother (Sacks, 2017) as described above and on Ted talk by Sacks (2018). Zimmerman

(2018) refers to Athan's revival of the term and wrote, "The term deliberately evokes the passage into adulthood — adolescence — though the two aren't exactly on equal footing in our collective consciousness".

The Cambridge Dictionary (2019) added an entry for *matrescence* as a specialised social science term that describes "the process of becoming a mother: Those physical, psychological and emotional changes you go through after the birth of your child now have a name: matrescence".

Dana Raphael (1975, cited in www.pbbmedia.org and www.matrescence.com) described the term *matrescence* in the following way.

> The critical transition period which has been missed is matrescence. the time of mother-becoming…Giving birth does not automatically make a mother out of a woman…The amount of time it takes to become a mother needs study.

Similar to Raphael (1975), Athan and Reel (2015) too highlighted the need to develop the emerging field of maternal psychology and situated the framework for and of matrescence, the transition to motherhood at the intersection of feminism and developmental psychology. Sacks (alexandrasacksmd.com, 2018) described *matrescence* in the following way.

> The birth of a mother involves similar hormonal and identity transitions to adolescence, and yet this natural process is often silenced by shame or misdiagnosed as postpartum depression. Perhaps instead we should be giving it a name: matrescence.

Sacks and Birndorf (2019), the reproductive psychiatrist, described the term by situating her research at the intersection of biochemical and developmental psychology.

> …descriptions of discomfort are natural to matrescence, and not diagnostic of any specific disease. It's no coincidence that matrescence sounds like adolescence. Both are times when body morphing and hormone shifting lead to an upheaval in how a person feels emotionally, and how they fit into the world. And like adolescence, matrescence is not a disease, but since it's not in the familiar medical vocabulary, it's being confused with a serious condition (that deserves its own expanded outreach, research, and advocacy) called Postpartum Depression.

Please note that while Identity is a major theme of this model and according to key figures within this field an encompassing transition is what a woman goes through as she becomes mother, this discussion is not to be confused with or to be used to conceptualise serious mental health condition such as postpartum depression.

"Motherhood mindset" ... identity

Also worth noting that Stern (2001) and Sack (2017) both psychiatrists who have dedicated their lives to working with mothers are trained in researching a field that has remained less explored and are trained in Psychoanalysis. They seem to be drawing theoretical framework from a field that prioritises individuality. Their training and theories seem to focus on the mother and the impact a child or a concept of child may have on the mother. Their articulation seems to come from a discipline that allows the clinician to go beyond the usual individual popular psychological theories that explain the general "mindset" or "psychological make up" or personality type of a person. A field that goes beyond the usual psychological theories that are centred upon the mother-child dynamics, offering parenting insights/tips but not particularly shedding light on the maternal transition of the woman. Based on Stern's (2001) and Sack's (2017) work psychoanalysis seems to be that field at least when it comes to the transition of a woman to motherhood. This is confirmed by Stern (2001) as he reflected on his clinical experience of working with mothers and highlighted how general psychological theories do not resemble his clinical experience.

> ...members of the psychological community have relied on accepted theories when working with mothers. Most psychological theories are based on general principles that apply to a broad spectrum of people and the ways their minds function...I... realize that the traditional psychological models did not accommodate the influence of motherhood on a woman's mindset...the uniqueness of the motherhood was a revelation.
>
> (Stern, 2001, pp. 4–5)

Stern (2001) further clarified as to why he believed that the general psychological theories fall short in explaining the phenomena of becoming a mother.

> Our mindsets organize our mental lives to make us the coherent individuals we are. Depending upon the orientation of a mental health professional, he or she will ... use these theories to help a person understand his own mindset. No matter what theory is subscribed to, however, in none of them is motherhood viewed as anything but a slight variation on the already existing mindset. Noone thought that a woman's mental life could fundamentally change with the arrival of a baby.
>
> (Stern, 2001, p. 5)

Stern (2001, p. 4) is referring to a concept called the "Motherhood Mindset" which he coined in the opening pages of his book as he wrote,

> The motherhood mindset is not born at the moment the baby gives its first cry.
> The birth of a mother does not take place in one dramatic, defining moment...
> What produces this motherhood mindset? How is it unique to each woman, yet shared by all mothers? What phases does it pass through? And how can you

identify the passages of this remarkable new inner realm and learn to navigate its waters? … We start at the beginning: Who exactly is a mother, and is she inherently different from other women? … it strikes at the most basic assumptions held by the psychological and therapeutic communities.

Considering the above contribution from some of the key figures from within this small field of specialised clinical expertise, it seems that irrespective of the clinician's theoretical background and training, asking the client open phenomenological questions such as *how do they conceptualise motherhood* or *what is motherhood to them* would allow the client to explore their own position in relation to this transition. This type of questioning will also open up a pathway to further exploring the sub-themes within this theme explored below. Important to highlight that these are possible pathways of *exploration* only. The *type* of exploration will vary depending on the individual case and context. The types of questioning and/ or the needs of exploring a particular topic will also vary as they are dependent on the therapist's clinical judgements. However, below are some examples of the areas that the sub-themes aim to explore.

a. Physical identity

Exploring this theme may mean enquiring around the person's perception of their body, the physical changes that they went through or are currently experiencing as they transition to motherhood, including the expectation that others may have around them, the expectation of society in general, the ideals or presuppositions they themselves may have about their own physical self and the psychological impact of all of these factors on them. This is a significant sub-theme to explore considering the fact that pregnancy and childbirth bring in several significant changes to the human body some of which are temporary and others are permanent. This includes the person's perception of their postpartum body, physical impact of breastfeeding or not breastfeeding, exhaustion, hygienic changes in their routine or the lack of, changes in their body odour due to hormonal shifts and caring for the baby, physical experience of recovering from surgery or the birthing process, seeking to get back to their usual physical sense of self, changes in their clothing styles due to sizing or other issues, the limitedness that they may experience when opening their wardrobe and several other moments experienced by them in relation to their changing body and how it contributes to or impact their physical identity.

b. Social (friends and the wider world)

This theme refers to the enquiry of the person's identity in relation to their friends, associates, acquaintances and the wider world. This includes the changes in their existing relationship, their identity as a friend, their inability to attend social events same as before, other changes in their socialisation pattern and process in general, their comfort or discomfort around topics discussed before and/or after birth at social settings, their sense of identification and connection built and/or lost with others as they go through the transition and several other unique aspects experienced by them in relation to their social identity during their perinatal period.

c. Intimate partner(s)/sexual

This sub-theme denotes the pathway to explore the person's sexual identity such as their sense of self in relation to sexuality, intimacy, intimate partner(s) or potential partner(s). Considering pregnancy, birth and parenting come with significant physical changes such as hormonal, muscular and gynaecological to name a few, especially if the person is breastfeeding in the postpartum period, it is important to explore this theme if the clinician feels there is a scope for exploring. The desire to be desired or even desiring another human being in an intimate or sexual manner may seem foreign to some during this period. While others may be longing to return to their pre-pregnancy level of sexual connections and/or intimacy but experiencing physical, environmental and psychological barriers. Some may also be looking to rebuild and/or redefine their sexual relations and/or intimacy during this period. Others may be experiencing unique challenges of their own.

d. Productivity/employment/economic

This sub-theme is meant to explore the person's identity as part of the workforce or the financial infrastructure they believe they are situated within. Often as she embarks on the journey of becoming a mother, some may think in their darkest hours that the only object she is producing at the moment is bodily fluid such as breastmilk! For instance, professional females may experience the perinatal period a sharp contrast to their previous life. She may be reflecting on the time when she was producing the results of her professional skills and training at work, got acknowledged and paid for her labour, economically contributed to the society, had a career and her life had a different structure, different set of goals and aims. Compared to this, she may perceive her current identity as almost meaningless or worthless even though she may dearly love her child/children and does not devalue domestic labour or caring jobs in any shape or form. Exploring questions like, "what is it like to not work and not be attending her usual workplace" or "not having the usual structure" or "what is it like to not have a routine that she was used to have and rather be led by the routine demanded by this tiny little fragile human", would provide the person with an opportunity to reflect and gain clarity about their sense of identity (or the loss of it) as a member of the economic structure they are part of.

e. Within family perception

This sub-theme is meant to provide the person with an opportunity to articulate the complex family dynamics that she is a part of and the impact that it may have on her as she transitions to motherhood. This may include the reaction that others in the family have about her pregnancy and motherhood, the changes in others' perception of her, the comments or the judgements or the perceived changes in others' views of her that she feels impacting her. For instance, the person may be compared to their sibling's or cousin's or aunt or someone else's pregnancy or motherhood as they transition to motherhood. It can also be that it is only perceived by the person this way, but nothing was said or communicated to her. In that case, there may also be historical context. Her reaction may only be based on her perception of others as she may feel inadequate in comparison to their sibling or other family members due to the pre-existing family dynamics or historical context. This in turn may have impact on the perception of herself and her identity further as part of the family unit she belongs to.

Supermom

It is imperative to highlight the obvious within the context of identity when it comes to perinatal mental health. We live in a world of constant emphasis on our image. We live in a world where we learn about the world from social media. A platform that has an infinite amount of information but very little knowledge. A world where everyone knows or at least claims to know everyone else's stories. But the facts and truth about our existence are filtered and packaged in this virtual world. A version of our life presented on screen that is nothing but untrue and bears almost no resemblance to reality at times. The social discourse on motherhood is currently promoting a very different idea of what a mother should and should *not* be like. This is a very different discourse than the last 10 years or 20 years or even prior to that. It is important that a clinician explores these differences. Such as what these differences mean to the client; are the clients even aware of the differences in the standard of motherhood and that it has not been static but rather revolving, changing over time and changing almost into something that is unattainable; the person will benefit from having the invitation from their therapist to explore the feeling of constant pressure and frustration which they may feel from their time of scrolling on social media. A pressure to perform a type of motherhood that is essentially unrealistic but they aim for it anyway. A level of constant frustration and inadequacy thinking "everyone" else is doing it *right*, doing it *all,* and only they can not…! Alexander Sacks steered clear from this *argumentum ad populum* and further debunked the "Instagram-supermom" myth. While most social media platforms, celebrity news and the advertising sectors are trying to portray a particular " norm" of motherhood, Sacks wrote the following.

> supermom: a nurturing, organized, sexy-but-modest multitasker who glows during prenatal yoga and seems unfazed by the challenges of leaking breasts, dirty laundry and sleep training. This woman is a fiction.
>
> (Sacks, 2017)

Conclusion

This chapter provided an outline of some of the major clinician's account and theories on maternal identity during the perinatal period from this small specialised clinical field. The theme of identity and its sub-themes were explored. The chapter also highlighted some possible open phenomenological questions that therapists can ask their clients irrespective of the clinician's theoretical background and training. The next chapter will explore the theme "Idea of motherhood/fatherhood – femininity/masculinity".

References

APA. (2023). *American Psychological Association dictionary of psychology* (online). Retrieved April 10, 2023, from: https://dictionary.apa.org

Athan, A. (2023). *Matrescence: Education and theory and practice*. Retrieved April 10, 2023, from https://www.matrescence.com/

Athan, A., & Reel, H. L. (2015). Maternal psychology: Reflections on the 20th anniversary of *deconstructing developmental psychology*. *Feminism & Psychology*, *25*(3), 311–325. https://doi.org/10.1177/0959353514562804.

Cambridge Dictionary. (2019). *Matrescence*. Retrieved April 10, 2023, from https://dictionary.cambridge.org/dictionary/english/matrescence

Raphael, D. (1973). *Being female: reproduction, power and change. Editor Dana Raphael*. The Hague-paris: Mouton.

Raphael, D. (1975). Matrescence, becoming a mother, a "New/Old" rite de passage. In D. Raphael (Ed.), *Being female: Reproduction, power, and change* (pp. 65–72). De Gruyter Mouton. https://doi.org/10.1515/9783110813128.65

Sacks, A. (2022). *Alexandra Sacks M.D.* Retrieved April 9, 2023, from http://www.alexandrasacksmd.com/

Sacks, A. (2017, May 08). The birth of a mother. *The New York Times*. Retrieved April 9, 2023, from https://www.nytimes.com/2017/05/08/well/family/the-birth-of-a-mother.html

Sacks, A. (2018, May 11). Reframing 'Mommy Brain.' The New York Times. Retrieved from https://www.nytimes.com/2018/05/11/well/family/reframing-mommy-brain.html

Sacks, A., & Birndorf, C. (2019). *What no one tells you: A guide to your emotions from pregnancy to motherhood*. Orion Books.

Stern, D. (2001). *The interpersonal world of the infant.1985*. BasicBooks.

Sultana, M. (2018). *The castration complex: What is so natural about sexuality?* Routledge, Taylor & Francis Group.

Sultana, M. (2021). *Becoming a mother: A study of current and potential response to perinatal mental health* [Doctoral Thesis, UCD School of Medicine]. Retrieved April 4, 2023, from https://researchrepository.ucd.ie/bitstreams/42e5d42b-bba3-408f-acf2-283c48534da3/download

Zimmerman, E. (2018, May 25). *The identity transformation of becoming a mom*. Retrieved April 10, 2023, from https://www.thecut.com/2018/05/the-identity-transformation-of-becoming-a-mom.html

Chapter 5

Idea of Motherhood/Fatherhood – Femininity/Masculinity

Introduction

This chapter will first highlight the rationale for using this theme. The chapter will then provide some of the working definitions that are widely accepted in the clinical and research world for therapists' consideration to use as a starting point for exploring these themes with their clients.

What comes to mind when I say mother/father?

The idea of motherhood and fatherhood is a major theme that will be explored below. These are concepts that may seem straightforward from the outset as they are part of our daily life. Yet when the participants (midwives) of my Doctoral research study and every perinatal mental health workshops I have ever conducted with allied health professionals were asked to define these terms, they all responded very differently. What does that tell us? We all have our unique perception and conceptualisation of motherhood and fatherhood. Our individuality and our experiences on this planet shape our relationships with these concepts. Similarly, the ideas of what is it to be a woman or a man, the binary ideas of gender, the questions of femininity and masculinity are also complicated terms. We all have our unique way of conceptualising them. So no matter how simple they may seem on the surface, these are complex ideas that we all define differently, somewhat uniquely like our own fingerprints! Similarly, the impact that these words may have on us, on our psyche, especially during the perinatal period, is also going to be unique. It is essential to explore these terms with perinatal clients in therapy rather than assuming any aspect of it. As clinical experience has taught me, sometimes and in fact most times, it may be the only time in their life that the person was ever asked these questions or given the opportunity to reflect on them. Such invitation to reflect offers them to articulate something that they themselves never quite put words to it, but was somewhat aware of their existence in their mind.

Below are the two examples of results from workshops I have conducted with professionals. Participants were either medical doctors or allied health professionals attending training events for specialist perinatal mental health. They were asked

DOI: 10.4324/9781003309710-6

to reflect on the question "what is a mother". They were asked to focus on what does the word "mother" remind them of. They were then asked to write their answers freely and anonymously on a shared interactive webpage. Similarly, they were asked to reflect on the question "what is a father?" And they were asked to share their answers similarly focusing on what comes to their mind when the word "father" is mentioned. Notice the variety of responses that these professionals gave as illustrated in the word clouds below.

As Figures 5.1 and 5.2 illustrate, we all have very different ideas and presuppositions about what these terms mean. The main aim of the clinician when working with this theme is to create a safe and open space for the individual to explore these so-called regular terms or "everyday knowledge" as they may not get another opportunity to explore them outside the therapy sessions. The rationale is that these terms are intricately connected to our presuppositions and expectations about the world and about ourselves. Our dreams, hopes, values and roles are shaped internally by the way these terms are conceptualised by us, both consciously and unconsciously. Especially, the unconscious ideals, biases, theories and presuppositions contribute to the construction of gender in our minds. Such construction has an impact on our actions. Operating both at the surface and underneath a person's conscious mind, these constructions may contribute to the psychological difficulties related to the question of becoming a mother/father. Hence exploring them with the person allows the person to see their own presuppositions and connections, helping them become much more aware of their inner world.

Definitions ... a starting point

For the purposes of this model, these terms are being used in the same sense as it is described in the American Psychological Association's (APA) Dictionary

Figure 5.1 What comes to mind when I say "Mother".

Source: Author

Figure 5.2 What comes to mind when I say "Father".
Source: Author

(see below). However, that is only the starting point of the discussion, as it is recommended that the therapist opens up a dialogue with their client, using the most common definitions of these terms and invites them to explore these concepts further as part of this theme. As mentioned before, clinical experience has taught me that most clients appreciate these opportunities. Being able to explore them with a therapist who is equipped with the specialist knowledge of the perinatal mental health helps the client learn a lot about themselves that they never thought they had in them. A therapist willing to work as a specialist within the perinatal mental health world must know the significance of these terms and about the potential impact they may have on the person's psyche, especially during their perinatal period. There are several ways to describe these terms, but below are the definitions from the APA Dictionary as guiding points for leading the discussion with clients should the clinician chooses to do so. Please note that the APA Dictionary does not have some of these terms in the form that they are presented above. The closest equivalents that are available on the APA website are captured below.

"Femininity": "possession of social-role behaviors that are presumed to be characteristic of a girl or woman, as contrasted with femaleness, which is genetically determined" (APA, 2023).

"Masculinity": "possession of social role behaviors that are presumed to be characteristic of a boy or man, as contrasted with maleness, which is genetically determined" (APA, 2023).

"Femaleness": "the quality of being female in the anatomical and physiological sense by virtue of possessing the female complement of a pair of X chromosomes" (APA, 2023).

"Maleness": "the quality of being male in the anatomical and physiological sense by virtue of possessing the XY combination of sex chromosomes" (APA, 2023).

Considering how complex it is to define what a mother is, note that "Mothering" according to the APA Dictionary is as follows: "the process of nurturing, caring for, and protecting a child by a mother or maternal figure" (APA, 2023).

Interestingly, there is no equivalent of "Mothering" in the APA Dictionary for the opposite sex. There is no entry for "Fathering". Considering how complex and unique it is for any of us to define what a father is, it is essential to explore this term with clients during the perinatal period no matter what gender they identify as.

Considering the vastness of the topic of sex, gender and identity, exploring these terms in detail is beyond the scope of this book. I have explored these terms elsewhere questioning the "natural" aspect of sexuality using psychoanalytic theories (Sultana, 2018) and as part of my Doctoral research that focused on building the theoretical framework to conceptualise the transition to motherhood (Sultana, 2021). For clinicians who are interested in exploring these terms with their clients as part of this theme from a social science perspectives and not just from a psychological perspective, below are some relevant definitions that can serve as a starting point of discussion.

In the International Encyclopaedia of the Social & Behavioral Sciences, Kimmel (2001) described "Masculinities" and "Femininities" in plural, in the following way.

Masculinities and femininities refer to the social roles, behaviors, and meanings prescribed for men and women in any society at any time. Such normative gender ideologies must be distinguished from biological 'sex,' and must be understood to be plural as there is no single definition for all men and all women. Masculinities and femininities are structured and expressed through other axes of identity such as class, race, ethnicity, age, and sexuality. Thus some definitions are held up as the hegemonic versions, against which others are measured. Gender ideologies are more than properties of individuals; masculinities and femininities are also institutionally organized and elaborated and experienced through interactions.

In the International Encyclopaedia of the Social & Behavioral Sciences (Second Edition), Windsor (2015) described "Femininity" as below.

'Femininity' is a familiar term. Conversations about being feminine are common in everyday life and many people use the word 'feminine' to describe themselves and others. They may equate femininity with being a woman who embodies characteristics like being nurturing, sensitive, demure, or sweet. But femininity cannot be understood as a fixed set of essential traits that characterize all women. As a scholarly concept, femininity can carry diverse meanings with numerous interpretations. Within the context of heterosexual relationships, performances of femininity can employ different scripts. These scripts act as guidelines for individual behavior and social interaction. They are learned at an early age and reinforced throughout the life course.

When examined as a whole, individual expressions of femininity reveal distinct patterns. These themes become reinforced throughout different social institutions such as media, education, religion, sports, and the workforce. Studying these institutional or macro level forms makes it possible to see how ideas about femininity represent a much larger concept than simply wearing makeup and high heels while smiling coyly and sitting with one's legs crossed.

In the Encyclopaedia of Mental Health (Second Edition), Mankowski and Smith (2016) described "Masculinity" in the following way.

Masculinity is a form of gender, variously defined as an identity, a social role, and a form of power and is typically, though not exclusively, associated with men. In the socialization of masculinity, boys and men are encouraged to reject or avoid anything stereotypically feminine, to be tough and aggressive, suppress emotions (other than anger), distance themselves emotionally and physically from other men, and strive toward competition, success and power. In particular, anti-femininity and homophobia are at the core of what traditional masculinity means. Boys and men are rewarded in a variety of settings such as schools, intimate relationships, the workplace, military, and prisons for adhering to these stereotypic expectations and often are punished or rejected for violating them. However, fulfillment of these gendered expectations is also associated with a range of health and social problems including anxiety and depression, substance abuse, and interpersonal violence.

The above serve as a guiding point to start a discussion on these topics with persons attending perinatal counselling. It is ultimately the clinician's decision as to which perspective is more appropriate for the client to open this discussion based on a number of factors as they consider relevant. However, clinical experiences have taught me that the level of therapeutic alliance built with the client and the point where the client is on their therapeutic journey in therapy are crucial factors to consider before inviting the person to a dialogic process around these terms.

Conclusion

This chapter has explored complex terms such as mother, father, femininity, masculinity and more in order to highlight how the subjective element of these terms. The chapter also emphasised on the importance of exploring them with perinatal counselling clients as they impact the person's psyche mostly unknowingly. The next chapter will explore the major theme "Loss" (symbolic).

References

APA. (2023). *American Psychological Association dictionary of psychology* (online). Retrieved from: https://dictionary.apa.org Retrieval date 4 April 2023

Kimmel, M. (2001). Masculinities and femininities. In N. J. Smelser & B. Baltes (Eds.), *International encyclopedia of the social and behavioral sciences* (pp. 9318–9321). Elsevier.

Mankowski, E., & Smith, R. (2016). Men's mental health and masculinities. *Encyclopedia of Mental Health*, 66–74. https://doi.org/10.1016/b978-0-12-397045-9.00182-8

Sultana, M. (2018). *The castration complex: What is so natural about sexuality?* Routledge, Taylor & Francis Group.

Windsor, E. J. (2015). Femininities. *International Encyclopedia of the Social & Behavioral Sciences*, 893–897. https://doi.org/10.1016/b978-0-08-097086-8.35015-2

Sultana, M. (2021). Becoming a mother: A study of current and potential response to Perinatal Mental Health (dissertation). University College Dublin, Dublin.

Chapter 6

Loss (Symbolic)

Sub-themes:

a Identity
b Freedom
c Personal space/privacy/alone time
d Spontaneity
e Social life/leisure
f Desire/desirability

Introduction

This chapter explores loss as a major theme of the Becoming model and its related six sub-themes. The main aim of this chapter is to highlight the complex nuances of loss experienced by the person both at an intra-personal and inter-personal level contributing to psychological difficulties related to the question of becoming a mother/father. The chapter also provides exploring techniques by highlighting major definitions of some of the terms used in this chapter as conversation starter with the perinatal clients in counselling.

A symbolic loss

This theme focuses on the sense of loss experienced by the person during pregnancy and post partum despite giving birth to a healthy offspring. As I started my research in this area, I found that possibly the only sense of loss captured in most of the official documents related to health care within this field focused on pregnancy loss and stillbirth. The focus in those literature is on actual loss or bereavement experienced by the person during the perinatal period. The landscape of perinatal mental health in Ireland today has drastically transformed since 2018 as the Specialist Perinatal Mental Health team has been established and is in operation. Prior to that, the focus on maternal mental health was comparatively less following a healthy delivery in Ireland. Moreover, the official documents from pre 2018 that provide guidelines for care seemed to not have included or captured the sense of loss that a clinician witnesses in their perinatal clients. In other words, maternal mental health seemed to have gotten attention when there was an actual loss. Whereas a sense of symbolic loss despite a healthy birth is witnessed by most therapists within a counselling session with perinatal clients. For instance, *The National Maternity Strategy* by the Health Service Executives (HSE) (HSE, 2016a, 2016b) was a 133 paged document which mentioned perinatal mental health in just over one page at paragraph 3.9 (2016b, pp. 61–62). However, the document titled *Bereavement Care Following Pregnancy Loss and Perinatal Death* published by the HSE in 2016 (reviewed in 2019) was a 86 paged document. There are several

DOI: 10.4324/9781003309710-7

explanations for this contrast. However, the two major questions that occurred to me within the context of therapeutic engagement were the following.

- Is perinatal *mental health* at all considered by the service providers in cases where pregnancy loss and/or bereavement is absent?
- Do service providers within this field tend to associate a felt sense of loss experienced by the service users only when an actual loss of a foetus or a child takes place?

The fact that much before the Diagnostic Statistical Manual (DSM) (American Psychiatric Association [APA], 2017) included Depression with Peripartum Onset, Postnatal Depression became a household term indicating something worth highlighting. As mortal and fragile humans, we knew much before the "Masters" declared it as an official term that something can and does happen at childbirth. The manifestation of which is a significant disturbance experienced by the person, even where there has not been a death or bereavement. That one can experience a loss of "something", even when mother and baby seem healthy. Similarly, anyone working therapeutically within this field would attest to the very fact that when it comes to experiencing a sense of "loss" within the perinatal period, it is not just limited to the experience of losing a life and/or foetus and/or embryo and/or zygote. In some cases, women may experience a sense of loss or emptiness in their own bodies after a healthy delivery. A sense of missing the bump or missing the child residing so intimately for nine months, loss of feeling connected to the child, a sense of loss or as if something is missing, a feeling of emptiness right under their skin! However, in other cases, the sense of loss is much more symbolic and abstract. Thus the proposal made to the clinicians working within this field is to conceptualise this sense of loss using a wider lens. A lens that accommodates the perception of loss that goes much beyond an actual loss of a baby or a foetus. It is also clinically more appropriate and useful to conceptualise the experience of "becoming a mother" as a phenomenon that includes an experience of multidimensional loss. The manifestation of such felt sense of loss will be unique and will vary widely from person to person. In other words, the person may experience a sense of symbolic loss unique to their situation during the perinatal period in relation to a number of different aspects of their life. So it is important that the therapist is aware of and explores these aspects with their clients. Some of the most prominent ones are captured here under this theme as sub-themes.

a. Identity

Chapter 4 outlined the theme of "Identity" and its sub-themes in detail. "Identity" as a sub-theme in this chapter within the theme of "Loss" is to be explored with an emphasis on loss. Such as loss of the person's sense of identity. For instance, most of us introduce ourselves within a group scenario by firstly using our name, then our location (where we are from) and/or by our profession or the work we do. Hence, our name, origin and professions/work are the most integral parts of our sense of identity. There are several other aspects of our life that help us build a sense of identity such as the groups we belong to such as our nationality, ethnicity, religion, hobbies, our social status, professional groups and other social groups that we are part of to name a few. However, our sense of identity may be hampered in our mind as we transition to motherhood. For instance, soon after one becomes pregnant, they begin to realise that the changes occurring in their body will impact their intimate relationship(s), social relationships and their employability. Instead of a partner or a wife or a shop assistant or an accountant or a CEO, they are now a mother who is responsible for this tiny fragile human being 24/7 without entitled breaks or a recognition or a bonus or any option of an annual review with a view to promotion! Clinical experience would attest to the fact that such awareness in most cases does not automatically mean that they are not happy or regret being a mother. Rather, this is a different identity or rather they become aware of the loss of their previous identity, even though it may be a temporary situation. So they might interpret their identity as someone who instead of producing money and so-called "meaningful contribution" to the society, now produce milk! The loss of ability to produce money, the loss of one's financial identity and professional identity and how they impact the person – these are the most important aspects to explore when considering this sub-theme.

Please note that this sense of loss in one's identity is independent of the person's desire to have a child. It may be tempting to draw simplistic conclusions based on seemingly rational assumptions that those who desire to be pregnant will not experience this sense of identity loss. However, clinical experience will show that in reality even the cohort of mothers who go through their much-anticipated pregnancy by opting for various assisted reproductive treatment options, such as donor eggs, surrogacy or IVF to name a few, experience a sense of loss in their identity in the postpartum period. Even when the outcome was planned and the person has been preparing for years, they may experience this sense of loss of identity.

While this sense of loss does not clinically get presented in the same way, underneath the symptoms there maybe a question of loss of identity in most cases. For instance, a successful graphic designer on maternity leave after a much-awaited pregnancy may wish to extend their maternity leave and take unpaid leave knowing that they may suffer financial difficulties and miss out on a much-awaited promotion at work. They may decide so quite willingly. This does not mean that they do not experience a sense of loss in their identity or question the future of their career. They may willingly stay back from work and worry about when and how to return to work. They may worry about under whose care will they leave this tiny human. They may also decide to return to work and continue to feel a sense of loss of identity as a huge sense of guilt sets in. In most cases, the guilt maybe around the sense of a perceived abandonment, such as leaving their baby at home or at daycare with someone else and returning to work. They may oscillate between feeling a loss of identity as the graphic designer and the mom. These are situations where the person usually begins to question their identity as they are unsure about who they really wish to be – a mother or a career-orientated employee. This dilemma or binary choice begins to often torment the person. This is especially problematic as we live in a society where a female-bodied person is often expected to choose their child over career, and hence an added layer of shame and guilt sets in as they question their identity or the lack of it. It is essential to highlight that this sense of loss is not to be equated with or interpreted as the person's lack of love for the new baby. Rather the therapist must help them make sense of this loss as a natural phenomenon in their own preferred ways. However most importantly needs to be communicated that a sense of loss of identity is an integral part of becoming a mother, that multiple senses of identities can coexist alongside and that there is no correlation between their sense of loss of identity and their love for the child or their desire to be a mother. One does not automatically negate or reduce the other.

b. Freedom

This sub-theme is meant to provide a pathway for the therapists to help their clients explore the felt experience of loss of freedom. Below are some of the major sources of definition for this term that can be used as a starting point for the discussion within the therapeutic clinic.

Freedom according to the Britannica Dictionary is as follows (Britannica, 2010):

1 The state of being free, such as

   a The power to do what you want to do: the ability to move or act freely
   b The state of not being a slave, prisoner, etc.
   c The state of not having or being affected by something unpleasant, painful, or unwanted – + *from*
   d freedom from care
   e freedom from pain/fear
   f freedom from responsibility
   g The right to use something or go somewhere without being controlled

2 A political right

Freedom according to the Collins Dictionary "is the state of being allowed to do what you want to do" (Collins, 2007).

Freedom according to the Oxford Dictionary is as follows (Oxford, 1992):

• The power or right to do or say what you want without anyone stopping you
• The state of not being a prisoner or slave
• The state of being able to move easily
• The state of not being affected by the thing mentioned (e.g., freedom from pain/ fear)
• Permission to use something without limits

Freedom according to the Cambridge Dictionary is as follows (Vale et al., 1996):

- The condition or right of being able or allowed to do, say, think, etc., whatever you want to, without being controlled or limited
- A right to act in the way you think you should
- A state of not being in prison

While motherhood can be a blessing and a life-altering experience in a beautiful way, it can also be a reminder of several limitations that the person may experience during their perinatal period. For instance, the person may literally experience a loss of freedom of movement as they progress in their pregnancy and as their body changes. They may especially experience loos of freedom movement post-delivery as they recover from the birth or C-section. Moreover, if they are breastfeeding, they usually have limited number of hours that they can be away from their child as their engorged painful breasts will provide them with a timely reminder that they need to return to the baby or use a breast pump. These are just some of the obvious ways that a person may sense a lack of freedom. A sense of being tied that they can cherish and love on one hand as they feel connected and blessed. But also limited in their sense of freedom and a sense of loss on the other hand. These feelings can co-exist. However, when explored in a safe space with empathy, a clinician can help the person dive deep into several other complex instances of experiencing the feeling of loss of freedom that are unique to the person and that may be connected to the sense they are experiencing during their perinatal period.

c. Personal space/privacy/alone time

This sub-theme refers to the person's perceived experience of a loss of personal space. For example, the journey of becoming a mother includes a temporary loss of space in one's bed as the child often spends the early weeks and months of their life in their parents' bed and/or bedroom. It may also include a loss of alone time for the mother/father/parent as one cannot just leave the baby behind to take a bath or carry out their usual hygienic routine or even have couple's time alone whenever they wish. At times the person may also experience a loss of privacy as sometimes mothers/fathers/parents have no other option but to carry their babies with them to the bathroom.

d. Spontaneity

This sub-theme refers to the person's perceived experience of a loss of ability and opportunities to be spontaneous with their plans like they used to or were able to, before the pregnancy and before they became a mother/father/parent. For instance, a trip to the cinema, social visits, weekend getaways or even trips to the grocery store usually have to be planned well in advance for most new parents. Exploring with the person the impact of these changes in their life in a safe space will help the person gain clarity and awareness about their emotions.

e. Social life/leisure

This sub-theme refers to the person's perceived experience of a loss of social life and leisure activities. In most cases during the perinatal period, the person's social life goes through a massive transition. For instance, they may not be able to do their usual meet-ups with their existing friends as much as they used to after they become a mother/father/parent. They may also not feel connected or interested in meet-ups with their previous friends and acquaintances as they may have very little in common with them after the birth of their child. Similarly, the person's leisure activities may also go through a transformation. They may lose interest and/or lose opportunities to continue with their leisure activities and hence experience a sense of loss.

f. Desire/desirability

This sub-theme refers to the person's perceived experience of a loss of desire and/ or desirability. In most cases, pregnancy and childbirth impact the person's desire in many ways. Especially, after a C-section it takes at least 8–10 weeks or longer for some women to enjoy penetrative sex. Moreover, the changes that a woman's body goes through during pregnancy, birth and post birth impact the person's perceived desirability. For instance, most women become conscious about changing their clothes in front of their partners post birth. They may experience a sense of discomfort that is often associated with a question about desirability. If they are breastfeeding, they may also feel uncomfortable about physical intimacy for a number of reasons that are unique to their context. A breastfeeding mother may also be questioning their desirability based on their own clothing which often in this case includes nursing bras and nursing-friendly clothing. Furthermore, a new mother's clothing is mostly covered in baby puke and milk, particularly her neck. A place once was the perfect target for spraying perfume or receiving a gentle kiss from their partner. She/he/they may also question their desirability as their body goes through other changes such as the aftermath of the pregnancy and the birth including different types of sensitivity, aches and discomfort. Most of these elements add to the questioning of the person's desire and desirability. In most cases, these are experiences that aren't talked about in theory unless there is a strong therapeutic alliance and the therapist is comfortable exploring these topics. However, having knowledge of this sub-theme is essential for facilitating this type of exploration. It helps the therapist create a safe space for the client to explore and articulate these experiences in a non-judgmental space.

Conclusion

This chapter explored symbolic loss as a major theme of the Becoming model and its related six sub-themes. The complex nuances of multidimensional loss experienced by the person can contribute to psychological difficulties during the perinatal period. It is essential that the therapist is aware of these complexities and invites the person to explore them while being guided by their own clinical judgement. The next chapter will explore the major theme "Experience of conception, pregnancy and birth".

References

APA. (2017). *Diagnostic and statistical manual of mental disorders: DSM-5*. American Psychiatric Association.

Britannica. (2010). Freedom. In *Britannica*. Encyclopaedia Britannica.

Collins. (2007). Freedom. In *Collins dictionary*. Collins.

HSE. (2016a). *National standards for bereavement care following pregnancy loss and …* Retrieved April 11, 2023, from https://www.hse.ie/eng/services/list/3/maternity/bereavement-care/national-standards-for-bereavement-care-following-pregnancy-loss-and-perinatal-death.pdf

HSE. (2016b). *National maternity strategy – creating a better future together 2016–2026*. Retrieved April 11, 2023, from https://www.gov.ie/en/publication/0ac5a8-national-maternity-strategy-creating-a-better-future-together-2016-2/

Oxford. (1992). Freedom. In *The Oxford dictionary*. Oxford University Press.

Vale, D., Mullaney, S., & Hartas, L. (1996). Freedom. In *The Cambridge dictionary*. Cambridge University Press.

Chapter 7

Experience of Conception, Pregnancy and Birth

Introduction

This chapter is dedicated to the theme of one's experience of conception, pregnancy and birth. The following sections will provide some basic information about the three major elements of the perinatal period: Conception, pregnancy and birth. The main aim of this chapter is to highlight the complexities of these elements and remind therapists that everyone's experience of these elements is very different. However, for the purposes of building therapeutic alliance and holding some common knowledge, the chapter will also provide quick outline of relevant terminologies and complications of each of these areas.

Conception

Counselling related to or during the time of conception usually falls within the field of fertility counselling. Including the time period that is before or around conception into the scope of perinatal counselling, there will now be an overlap between the two fields. Fertility counselling is an emerging field, and anyone who is interested in learning more in-depth about this topic would benefit from engaging with scientific literature from the field of fertility counselling. The following does not claim to define the field of fertility counselling in its true form and does not aim to do so either. Rather, the following is aimed at highlighting the most common terminologies or difficulties experienced by a person during their time of conception within the context of perinatal counselling. These terms are now situated in the intersection of perinatal counselling and fertility counselling with the scope of perinatal counselling proposed in this book.

While it is not necessary for a therapist to study medical terminologies to be able to explore them with their clients, it however helps the therapist connect with their clients more if the therapist is familiar with the most common terminologies within this field. While this is not a sub-theme on its own, exploring the person's experience of conceiving the child provides the therapist with a broad range of information that can help the therapeutic process. For the purposes of this discussion, the following will only focus on the most common difficulties that one may face when it comes to conception.

DOI: 10.4324/9781003309710-8

Fertility difficulties... terminologies

Difficulties in conceiving are often referred to as "fertility problems". This phrase would mean that a couple is having unprotected sex regularly but they are not conceiving. Fertility problems are also referred to as "infertility" or "subfertility". What seems to be a major clinical consideration within this context is that the therapist must tread carefully in relation to the language or phrasing used by them in the session when exploring the person's experience of difficulties with conception. Some clients may be sensitive to the term "infertility" and be more open to the phrase "difficulties with conception". Others may not be open with either phrases. It is up to the therapist to use their clinical judgement in using the appropriate language.

When a couple says they are "trying", they may be referring to having unprotected sex regularly, such as every 2–3 days. However, not all couples will be "trying" the same way or with the same frequency. Moreover, "trying" comes with its own sets of difficulties for the couple's relationship. The sense of hopelessness for both, a sense of intimacy becoming mechanical, a sense of loss of warmth and meaning overall in the relationship are just some of the most common difficulties that a client may experience during this phase. It is estimated that in Ireland around 1 in 6 heterosexual couples experience infertility (HSE 2019). Approximately, 85% of couples conceive a child naturally after one year of trying and after two years, approximately 95% will conceive (HSE, 2019). There are several other pathways to parenthood when it comes to fertility treatment for both heterosexual and same-sex couples. Hence, it is important to not assume, and rather enquire and explore the person's experience of conception. Generally, there are four major types of artificial reproductive technologies – in vitro fertilization (IVF), intracytoplasmic sperm injection (ICSI), intrafallopian transfer (IFT) and frozen embryo transfer (FET). In recent times, some individuals/couples also use the services of surrogates, where the pregnancy is carried out by someone else, contracted by the person who does not carry out the pregnancy but looking to become a parent.

Pregnancy

The experience of pregnancy is unique for each person as they transition to motherhood. Each pregnancy is also unique for the same person. The usual signs and symptoms of pregnancy are outlined here for the purposes of this theme. Common knowledge of these signs and symptoms can serve as a starting point for conversation with clients. This information is in no manner comprehensive. It is always best practice to consult with the national health services guidelines of the country that the therapist is practising in. In case of Ireland, that body is the Health Services Executive (HSE), and for the UK, it is the National Health Service (HNS).

Some of the major early signs of pregnancy are missed periods, tender breasts, fatigue and nausea. As the pregnancy progresses, the person may also experience mood swings, bloating, cramping, aversion and/or attraction to certain types of food, nasal congestion, constipation, feeling warmer than usual, frequent urination, changes in hair and skin, backaches and more. The NHS (2021) highlighted the following as common health problems during pregnancy: Back pain, bleeding gums, headaches, indigestion and heartburn, leaking nipples, nosebleeds, pelvic pain, piles, stomach pain, stretch marks, swollen ankles, feet and fingers, sleep difficulties, thrush, vaginal bleeding and/discharge and weight gain.

Complications... terminologies

The following are the most common physical complications that can occur during pregnancy (CDC, 2023; HopkinsMedicine, 2019):

Anaemia – During pregnancy one may experience low iron as their body needs more iron for the developing baby. This is referred to as iron-deficiency anaemia, low healthy red blood cells.

Amniotic fluid complications – The fluid around the foetus within the amniotic sack can be too little or too much sometimes, causing complications such as preterm labour, breathing difficulties for mom (too much fluid), birth defect or stillbirth.

Diabetes – This is a disease where the body's ability to turn food into energy is impacted. People with type 1 and type 2 diabetes are at higher risk than those without diabetes of experiencing preterm birth, birth defects and stillbirth. There is also gestation diabetes, a third type of diabetes that women can develop during pregnancy who do not have diabetes outside pregnancy. Gestational diabetes can increase a person's risk of developing type 2 diabetes later in their life.

Ectopic pregnancy – This is when a foetus is developing outside the uterus such as in the fallopian tube or the pelvic or belly or the cervical canal.

Hypertension – High blood pressure itself is another common complication during pregnancy. Hypertension is a heart condition where one has high blood pressure. High blood pressure before pregnancy or before 20 weeks of pregnancy is referred to as "chronic hypertension". "Gestational hypertension" is when it occurs for the first time after 20 weeks of pregnancy.

Placental complication – During the pregnancy, the placenta is supposed to attach to the uterine wall. However, some may experience "placental abruption", this is when the placenta detaches from the uterine wall too soon. Others may experience "placenta previa", this is when the placenta is attached too close to or almost covering the opening of the uterus or the cervix.

Preeclampsia – This is a condition that involves complications involving high blood pressure. A more severe form of this condition is often referred to as eclampsia which may lead to seizures, coma and death.

Birth

Everyone's birthing process is unique despite the procedures, complications and outcomes involved. The key here is to develop an open conversation about the process that the person went through and provide them with an open and non-judgemental space that is free from any presuppositions or ideals.

Complications and terminologies

Usually there are four types of birthing processes according to the NHS (2020) – vaginal or normal birth, vacuum extraction birth, forceps delivery, and caesarean section. Each of these types of birthing processes comes with risks and may have complications. The following are the most common birthing complications overall according to the National Institute of Child and Health Development (NICHD, 2017):

- Labour that does not progress
- Perineal tears
- Umbilical cord-related problems such as getting wrapped around the baby's neck, etc.
- Foetal heart rate abnormalities
- Water breaking early
- Perinatal asphyxia (foetus not receiving enough oxygen in the uterus)
- Shoulder dystocia (baby's shoulder getting stuck during vaginal birth)
- Excessive bleeding

Labour can sometimes start before 37 weeks and sometimes may not even progress well after 40 or 42 weeks. Both situations come with risks of complications. Deliveries between 39 weeks gestational and 40 weeks and 6 days gestational are considered "full term". Deliveries on the 37th and 38th weeks are referred as "early term". Deliveries before 37 weeks are referred as "preterm" or "premature". Babies born alive before 37 weeks are referred to as "preterm". The World Health Organization (WHO, 2023) noted three types of preterm birth based on gestational age: Birth at less than 28 weeks of gestation is "extremely preterm", birth between 28 and 32 weeks of gestation is "very preterm" and birth between 32 and 37 weeks is "moderate to late preterm".

Birth can also be live or stillbirth. According to the Centres for Disease Control and Prevention (CDC, 2023), stillbirth is a death or loss of a baby before or at birth. "Stillbirth" and "miscarriage" both refer to pregnancy loss. In the US, pregnancy loss is the loss of the foetus before 20 weeks of gestation and stillbirth is the loss of the foetus after 20 weeks of gestation. Stillbirth can also be "early" if occurs during 20–27 weeks of gestation, "late" if occurs between 28 and 36 weeks of gestation or "term" if occurs between 37 and more gestational weeks.

The abovementioned information are only intended to provide quick outline for complex medical terminologies. It is expected that therapist do their own research into these terms before using them in therapy. The main aim of sharing these facts and terminologies is to remind the therapist that each conception, pregnancy and birth are different and unique. Hence, it is crucial that the person gets the opportunity to reflect and explore on the complex nuances of expectations, hopes and actual bodily experiences felt by them during and around the conception, pregnancy and birthing period. This also includes exploring the complications that may have been experienced. While quick outlines of major or common complications have been outlined above, the complications can be all uniquely experienced. Hence, the above is in no way comprehensive. One of the most significant outcome of complications in the perinatal period is pregnancy loss and/or stillbirth and/or bereavement. When any of this is experienced by a person, the reality is that the person did not get to experience the most common phenomena of this period: Coming home with a child in the arm from the hospital. This chapter did not focus on any of the complications in particular, including loss and bereavement. It is hoped that the therapist will use the clinical judgment and preferred style of communication to explore the possible ways that these experiences are felt by the person and highlight the nuances that are articulated at times and perhaps remained unspoken otherwise. These experiences will continue to operate both at the surface and underneath a person's conscious mind contributing to psychological difficulties related to the question of becoming a mother/father/parent. It is thus imperative for the therapist to be open and willing to learn from the client about their experience of these elements of the perinatal period.

Conclusions

This chapter explored the major theme of "Experience of conception, pregnancy and birth". The chapter highlighted some basic facts, common complications and terminologies about these areas. The main aim was to highlight that each person experiences these elements of the perinatal period uniquely. The experiences of these elements may add to perinatal mental health difficulties further. Exploring them in therapy will provide a space and opportunity for articulation that the person may not get anywhere else. The next chapter will explore the major theme of "Couple and/or co-parent relationship" and its related thirteen sub-themes.

References

CDC. (2023, February 08). *Pregnancy complications*. Retrieved April 11, 2023, from https://www.cdc.gov/reproductivehealth/maternalinfanthealth/pregnancy-complications.html

HopkinsMedicine. (2019, November 19*). Complications of pregnancy*. Retrieved April 11, 2023, from https://www.hopkinsmedicine.org/health/conditions-and-diseases/staying-healthy-during-pregnancy/complications-of-pregnancy

HSE. (2019). *Types of fertility problems*. Retrieved April 11, 2023, from https://www2.hse.ie/conditions/fertility/treatment/

NHS. (2020). *Types of birth*. Retrieved April 11, 2023, from https://www.uhd.nhs.uk/services/maternity/poole/types-of-birth

NHS. (2021). Common Health Problems in Pregnancy. Retrieved from https://www.nhs.uk/pregnancy/related-conditions/common-symptoms/common-health-problems/ April 11, 2023

NICHD. (2017). *What are some common complications during labor and delivery?* Retrieved April 11, 2023, from https://www.nichd.nih.gov/health/topics/labor-delivery/topicinfo/complications#

WHO. (2023). *Preterm birth*. Retrieved April 11, 2023, from https://www.who.int/news-room/fact-sheets/detail/preterm-birth

Chapter 8

Couple and/or Co-Parent Relationship

Sub-themes:

a   From two to threesome
b   Parenting style differences
c   Differences in values
d   Differences in world-views
e   Perspectives on religion/ideals/ideologies
f   Perspectives on division of chores
g   Communication style
h   Role orientation
i   Coping styles and abilities
j   Sexual/intimacy (dis)satisfaction
k   Decision on finances
l   Conflicts about child rearing
m   Family history of distress (including trauma)

Introduction

This chapter explores the major theme of couple relationship and/or co-parenting relationship and its related 13 sub-themes. This chapter aims to highlight that partner support and the sub-themes related to this theme are factors that need to be explored in perinatal counselling session as the therapist see fit in their therapeutic journey. This is because these factors have the potential to contribute to perinatal distress. The chapter also draws from latest research related to the topic and from reputable sources such as national and international health and allied health agencies to provide basic information about the topics that the therapist can't use as conversation starting point.

Transition of the relationship

The relationship of a couple goes through significant transition after a baby's arrival. The challenges of rearing a new human may lead some couples to learn new ways to respect, support and trust each other, develop their relationships further, and others faced with similar challenges may spiral downwards. The biggest challenge of all is exhaustion and/or lack of sleep. This is not mentioned as a separate sub-theme to explore with client as part of this theme in the Becoming model. This is because the clinical experience will attest that lack of sleep and/or exhaustion is a major issue that is omnipresent under every theme and sub-themes of this model. When exploring the sub-themes of this theme, it is clinically beneficial to highlight

DOI: 10.4324/9781003309710-9

to the clients the possible role of exhaustion and/or sleep in human functioning. Especially it is beneficial to communicate the impact lack of sleep and exhaustion may have on our cognitive functioning and interpersonal relationships, the two most relevant areas within the context of this theme.

Inclusivity ...

Please note that while the following is written from a perspective of a couple who have had a live birth, it is essential to also highlight that the couple (heterosexual and same-sex) may also be from a diverse relationship background such as polyamorous, they may also be not a couple and a single mother/parent/carer rearing the child with the help of a family member or a friend or someone else with whom they may or may not have sexual relationship. Furthermore, the following may also seem to be applicable for a first-time parent or a single-child family. These sub-themes are not restricted to the traditional couple situations only. The following is also applicable for parents with multiple children. This is because becoming a parent at different stages in life to different children are unique experiences and hence navigating their own relationship with partner(s) or other significant other(s) are also unique during these periods. It is up to the clinician to draw from these sub-themes to explore different areas of the person as they see fit.

a. From two to threesome

Most couples struggle to feel like a couple after the arrival of a baby. Much less time is spent together as a couple, and more time is spent with their baby and/or existing children as a family. This may also mean that they have no space in the bed anymore to turn or sleep the way they used to. Their closet and floor space may also be taken up by the new person's equipment and clothing. Overall, their space for two will turn into a space for three or more! While this may not seem as a problem to some, each couple would respond differently to this new transition.

b. Parenting style differences

Most couples would struggle to articulate these differences and yet everyone experiences these differences. Parenting style differences become the most obvious in situations such as comforting the child when they are crying and a lot of efforts have already been made to soothe the child. It may also be about the parent's preferences about how to or whether to address the child's cries at all during night or nap time. One may see it as a tantrum and may not give in to the child's demand, while the other may see it as an opportunity to bond and comfort. Or they may disagree in establishing bedtime routine. Or it may be that one parent seeks co-sleeping, while the other wants their marital bed back just for the two of them. There are always more than two ways of dealing with the situation and more ways to integrate the two seemingly polar opposite preferences. It is up to the therapist to make their own clinical judgement as to how to address these issues. However, the purpose of this theme is to remind the therapist of the importance of exploring this area with their client as they see fit.

As a guiding point for the discussion on parenting style, the therapist could use the following parenting styles: Authoritarian, authoritative, permissive parenting (Baumrind, 1971) and uninvolved parenting (Maccoby & Martin, 1983). Furthermore, Baumrind's (1991) concepts of "responsiveness" and "demandingness" could also serve as guiding points for this exploration. Below is a snapshot of the four major parenting styles for the therapist to use as a guiding point of this discussion.

- **Authoritarian parenting** style usually refers to a style of parenting where the parent prefers to exert high level of control over the child, is usually less responsive to the child's emotional needs, seems strict in their decisions, is highly demanding within the parent-child relationship and provides the child with almost no warmth.
- **Authoritative parenting** style usually refers to a style of parenting where the parent prefers to exert high level of control over the child but is usually also highly responsive to the child's emotional needs, seems strict but also fair in their decisions and despite being highly demanding within the parent-child relationship, they are reasonably warm towards the child.
- **Permissive parenting** style refers to a style of parenting where the parent prefers to exert low level of control or almost no control over the child, is usually also highly responsive to the child's emotional needs, seems very loving and sets almost no boundaries or rules, demands almost nothing within the parent-child relationship and provides the child with the highest level of warmth.
- **Uninvolved or absent parenting** style refers to a style of parenting where the parent prefers to exert low level of control or almost no control over the child, is highly non-responsive to the child's emotional needs, seems neglectful, sets almost no boundaries or rules, demands almost nothing within the parent-child relationship and provides the child with almost no warmth.

c. Differences in values

In almost every major school of psychotherapy there are theoretical equivalents to the "value theory": Human beings are governed by a set of values or beliefs and principles. The main aim of this sub-theme is to help provide the person with a space and an opportunity to identify and explore their core values, beliefs, principles and the differences in that of their partner's if any. These can influence the predisposed ideas and suppositions that a person may have about becoming mother/father/parent that often works as the guiding force or motivation behind their choices and actions. Especially this is where the clinician could explore the person's beliefs such as what the person considers that a mother should or should not do or what a father should or should not do. The differences in one's values and beliefs could add another layer of barrier or challenges in the couple's lives as they navigate through the journey to becoming a mother/father/parent.

d. Differences in worldviews

We all have our own particular ways of looking at life. Our own theories on why we are on this planet, the purpose of us being alive, the reason for us to have come to this world, the reason for us to exit the stage in the end and a way that we make sense of whatever happened or is happening to us in between. We all have our own sets of explanations of our experiences and rationale for our existence on this planet. Worldviews can be explained in many different ways, and it varies between discipline. It also varies within psychology and psychotherapy based on theorists and school. But overall, our worldviews are a combination of our ethical, moral, political, spiritual, scientific beliefs, perspectives and other ways to looking at and making sense of the world around us. Unless we get a punctured tyre or something becomes loose in our car, we usually do not become aware of that part of the car. Similarly, we are not always aware of our worldviews unless something stops working. The perinatal period is a time when the person may gradually discover several aspects of their life and their inner world that they were unaware of previously. The therapist can help them detangle their threads of thoughts and shine some light using this sub-theme as the differences in the couple's worldviews that can influence their choices and contribute to further difficulties during this period.

e. Perspectives on division of chores

This sub-theme is a reminder for the therapist to explore the person's experience of how the chores and duties around the house and the household are being divided among the caregivers since the arrival of the newest member. For instance, who is doing the dishes, who is in charge of laundry, who is vacuuming, who is cooking and how often, who is doing midnight feeds and who is doing the bottles including washing and sterilising, etc. Most couples do not really sit down and have these conversations beforehand. Rather the habits emerge mostly without conscious efforts, and the couple go along with the natural flow of life. However, in most cases during the perinatal period, these seemingly small insignificant matters lead to misunderstandings, resentments and arguments. This is the period when teamwork becomes a key to run the household and hence open communication and plannings become imperative. Especially if the mother or the primary carer has returned to work after the arrival of the new baby, they now have two full-time jobs: Employment and mothering. It is at this stage that planning between the couple is essential as they can begin to resent each other because of perceived unfair division of chores, unfair distribution of free time and unequal distribution of resources and amenities post arrival of the baby.

For instance, consider a couple who has not discussed as to how the house is going to be run as a new member is added or a second or a third or so on to the family and as one of them or both of them return to work. The person with the usual mothering duties will now have the mothering duties, several usual and new chores around the house as the number of members of the household has increased and a formal employment to mind. Their partner may help them with some of these, but as there is no formal talk about this, neither of them will know what to expect or what is expected of them. Hence, one might always clean up and continue doing most chores not knowing whether the other will at all pick up the unfinished chores and finish them and if so then when. This may mean that one partner is constantly burning out doing overtime, with little amount of sleep, little time left for personal hygiene or leisure or social engagements, while they witness the other person managing to get their sleep, hygiene routine kept the same and continuing with their hobby and social engagements in some form, even if not same as before. There will be resentment between the couple, and there will be displaced and disproportionate responses in the house such as anger or other strong emotions that leave the atmosphere and the family more dissatisfied than before.

f. Perspectives on religion/ideals/ideologies

This sub-theme aims to explore the person's views and perspectives on religion, spirituality, ideals and ideologies. There are several ways to describe these terms, and the meanings will always have some individual elements to them. Hence, the therapist can introduce these concepts in several ways to begin the discussion. The importance lies in exploring these elements with the client as they may contribute towards distress experienced in the perinatal period. For the purposes of this model, the American Psychiatric Association (APA) dictionary entries for these terms can be used to begin the discussion.

Religion according to the APA dictionary refers to the following (APA, 2023).

> a system of spiritual beliefs, practices, or both, typically organized around the worship of an all-powerful deity (or deities) and involving behaviors such as prayer, meditation, and participation in collective rituals. Other common features of organized religions are the belief that certain moral teachings have divine authority, and the recognition of certain people, places, texts, or objects as holy or sacred.

Spirituality according to the APA dictionary refers to the following (APA, 2023).

1 A concern for or sensitivity to things of the spirit or soul, especially as opposed to materialistic concerns
2 More specifically, a concern for God and a sensitivity to religious experience, which may include the practice of a particular religion but may also exist without such practice
3 The fact or state of being incorporeal

Idealism according to the APA dictionary refers to the following (APA, 2023):

4 In philosophy, the position that reality, including the natural world, is not independent of mind Positions range from strong forms, holding that mind consti-
tutes the things of reality, to weaker forms, holding that reality is correlated with
the workings of the mind. There is also a range of positions as to the nature of
mind, from those holding that mind must be conceived of as absolute, universal,
and apart from nature itself to those holding that mind may be conceived of as
individual minds.
5 Commitment to moral, political or religious ideals

Ideologies according to the APA dictionary refer to the following (APA, 2023):

6 A more or less systematic ordering of ideas with associated doctrines, attitudes,
beliefs and symbols that together form a more or less coherent philosophy or
Weltanschauung for a person, group or sociopolitical movement
7 In Marxism, any philosophy or set of ideas is regarded as false and distorting,
usually because it ignores or tries to disguise the material basis of society

For instance, a couple may suddenly find themselves in uncomfortable positions
as they notice for the first time that they are not on the same page in relation to the
child's surname or their religion or their spiritual beliefs or whether the child will
undergo certain religious/social ceremony or whether they will have a faith at all
and if so what practices will they engage in or what language/dialect/accent should
the child have or what school should they attend or whether they should at all attend creche and school or should they be kept away from these institutions and
taught/socialised differently, etc. In most cases, the couple or the individuals do
not realise that these factors may lead to arguments, misunderstandings and resentment, especially if the couple have not talked about these before and more so if
there are already clear differences in their preferences and worldview.

g. Communication style

There are several theories on communication style. It is up to the therapist as to
which theory they will use to explore this theme that aligns best with their training
and preference. However, from the perspective of this model, it is important that
the therapist explores how the current communication style is impacting the couple
or the person and the significant others around them. As demonstrated above, this
period is when most families underestimate the value of clear communication and
suffer the consequences of miscommunication. Differences in communication style
can lead to further damage in the relationship. Becoming aware of one's own and
others' communication styles can make a world of difference for someone seeking therapy during the perinatal period. The following is one of the most common
theories within the literature of communication styles. Bourne (1995) outlined five

overarching communication styles: Aggressive, passive-aggressive, submissive, manipulative and assertive. Please note that it is unrealistic to imagine that humans can neatly fit into these categories. Everyone is different in their communication at some level. However, differences in communication styles can cause further disruption or miscommunication. The general traits present in someone's style of communication may contradict or seem as highly contrasting or almost incompatible to another's preferred style of communication. Often a couple or those who are co-parenting do not get to realise the differences in their communication styles until they are faced with difficulties and seek professional support in understanding their cross-connections. For instance, someone with an aggressive communication style living with someone with a submissive communication style may have found a way to keep peace until the perinatal period when their differences become highly contrasting to one another. Similarly, someone with an aggressive communication style living with someone with a passive-aggressive communication style might find themselves in a high-conflict situation faced with multiple stressors arising from various sources during the perinatal period. Furthermore, they may not even realise that they have different communication styles and that it is adding to their existing stressors. Hence, it is essential that the therapist addresses the persons' communication styles and how they are different or not in comparison to others around them. Table 8.1 is a synopsis of Bourne's (1995) theory highlighting the five overarching communication styles: Aggressive, passive-aggressive, submissive, manipulative and assertive.

Table 8.1 Five overarching communication style.

Aggressive	Passive-aggressive	Submissive	Manipulative	Assertive
Hostile	Indirectly aggressive	Avoids confrontation	Cunning	Socially and emotionally expressive
Intimidating	Sarcastic	Apologetic	Controlling	Protects own boundaries and respects others'
Bullying	Sulky	Soft volume (voice/behaviour)	Makes others feel obliged	Gets things done without hurting others
Dominant gesture	Patronising	Refuses compliment	Patronising	Accepts compliments
Loud volume (voice/behaviour)	Seemingly "sweet and innocent"	Does not express feelings or desire	Sulks to get others to fulfil needs	Speaks directly and open to the possibility of rejection
Threatening	Devious	Avoids responsibility and decision making	Speaks indirectly	Makes decisions and takes responsibility

Source: Adapted from Bourne (1995).

h. Role orientation

This sub-theme aims to explore the idea of how the new parents orient themselves into the new roles or position, namely "parenting". According to the APA Dictionary (2023), orientation has several meanings. The ones that are relevant to this sub-theme are mentioned below (APA, 2023):

8 The process of familiarising oneself with a new setting (e.g., a new home, neighbourhood, city) so that movement and use do not depend upon memory cues, such as maps, and eventually become habitual

9 An individual's general approach, ideology or viewpoint

10 The process of introducing a newcomer to a job, company, educational institution, or other environment

Becoming a mother/father/parent or a primary caregiver to a new life is a full-time job. A role that our society often does not view as "work". This is a role that is often devalued in comparison to the "work" produced in the traditional labour market. Care work that takes place within the domestic sector, especially between parent and child (including adult children to older parents), is often not valued or perceived the same way as traditional employment roles are for a number of reasons. Mainly because labour in the domestic sector does not produce money in return. However it *is* a job nonetheless that requires 24/7 shifts work; a role that does not come with any prospect of career progression or perks and benefits of regular employment; a role that people take up mostly out of love, hopefully unconditional love that is not dependent on any sense of return or profit. However, there is no formal orientation by Human Resources (HR) when one takes up this role. The person is meant to learn on the job on their own, while mostly being bombarded by others' opinions and experiences such as their friends, family, acquaintances and social media. The decline of religion and/or spirituality has left a vacuum of knowledge and guidance that can look up to or orient themselves with. Human civilisation is currently busy filling that vacuum with self-help books and thousands of filtered short videos on "how to" be a parent on social media. We are flooded with information but lacking knowledge. This is why role orientation is an important sub-theme to explore with the person as they get the opportunity to realise the basic fact that they have stepped into a role that no one told them how to do and what to aim for or achieve or manage. Parker (2007, p. 406) described this term as below.

> the concept of role orientation refers to how an individual defines their work role, such as how broadly they perceive their role; what types of tasks, goals, and problems they see as relevant to their role; and how they believe they should approach those tasks, goals and problems to be effective. Role orientation is a set of beliefs, and as such, is shaped by the environment, as well as by personality and individual differences.

While role orientation is a term that is highly relevant to the field of HR as evident above, it is worth translating into the field of perinatal counselling. Role orientation is a term that captures several aspects of how an individual defines and what they believe their role is and what is expected of them. That is essentially what a mother/father/parent lacks as they transition to motherhood/fatherhood.

i. Coping styles and abilities

Every individual deals with stress differently, and everyone has different abilities to cope with stress. This theme highlights the importance of exploring this topic because the awareness of these differences significantly contributes to the couple or the person's sense of well-being especially as they become a parent (again). Open discussion with their therapist helps them develop insight and clarity about the miscommunication and misunderstandings occurring at home during this crucial period.

There are several theories that clinicians can draw from in order to support them in exploring their client's preferred or natural ways of coping and client's abilities to deal with stress. This section will only highlight one such theory for the purpose of this model.

Bitter (1993) researched relational coping and formulated the following four categories of coping processes by adding pioneering family therapy theorist Virginia Satir's communication style (Satir, 1976) and contemporary Adlerian personality theorist Nira Kefir's Personality Priorities (Kefir, 1971). While of course no single human being can neatly fit into these categories, these are theoretical categories that can help the clinician identify certain patterns. Exploring coping styles in creative ways with clients in the perinatal period helps them see themselves and their partner(s) or significant others in a different light. Table 8.2 is an adapted version of the original table presented in Bitter's (1993) article. It highlights the theory of four major coping styles based on how one responds to stress and what they prioritise when experiencing stress. The following section will merge Satir's Stress position theories with Kefir's Personality Priorities and outline how each category may theoretically respond when in stress. The table represents four coping styles by combining Satir's Stress Position theory and Kefir's Personality Priorities. Each row represents a category of coping style. Each column indicates the distinctive features of the coping style.

1 **Placating-Pleasing**: This category may refer to individuals who are afraid of rejection, so they placate when they are highly stressed, saying mostly "yes" to no matter what others say and sacrifice themselves and their own positions, wishes, needs and wants. They usually struggle with their self-worth; they feel torn and pulled in from several directions as they put others ahead of them with the hope of pleasing them.
2 **Blaming-Significance**: This is the opposite end of placating-pleasing. These are individuals who will mostly blame others to preserve their self-worth. It is usually always someone else's fault but never theirs. They are mostly engaged

Table 8.2 Major coping styles. Adapted version of "Dysfunctional movements in response to stress" (Bitter, 1993).

Satir's Stress Position	Words	Feelings	Things they avoid	Price they pay	Kefir's Personality Priorities
Placating	Agreement	Anxiety	Rejection	Loss of identity/too many people to please	Pleasing
Blaming	Disagreement	Anger/irritation	Meaninglessness	Overworked/overburdened	Significance
Super reasonable	Rational	Irritation/fear to come out	Humiliation/ embarrassment	Social Distance	Control
Distracting	Irrelevant	Confusion	Pain/stress	Low productivity	Comfort

in strongly criticising others which maybe a cover-up for their tendency to criticise themselves. They usually complain about even small amount of stress and portrays a sense of having overworked or feeling the burden of the whole world on their shoulder. They are also highly likely to get annoyed and angry easily as they tend to feel irritated most of the time.

3 **Super reasonable-Control:** This category refers to individuals with personality who turns off their emotion and mostly operate from a position of logic and reason as if they are following algorithms like a computer. They mostly rely on structure, principles, emphasis on sounding smart and abstract, even if their communication seems inappropriate and even when it is at the cost of their own or other people's welfare. They always try to keep things under control as they do not want to seem stressed or vulnerable to others. They do so by controlling situations and people that they fear may result in them feeling embarrassed. This may lead to them usually feeling disconnected from others and social isolation.

4 **Distracting-Comfort**: This category refers to individuals who seek to not only maintain a sense of pleasure, but in stressful situation, they actively create distraction by resorting to doing anything in order to seek pleasure and comfort. Their efforts may seem irrelevant and disjointed as they usually try to distract people from the situation by saying literally anything which may be completely out of context and may even answer a question with a question.

In addition, it is not just one's coping style that is a mitigating factor to be considered here, but also it is imperative for the therapist to consider other predisposing factors that may influence or impact a person's or their partner's or significant other's ability to deal with stress. Becoming a mother/father/parent itself is a significant predisposing factor related to one's ability to manage stress. The situation becomes much more complicated when someone already has other predisposing factors present in their life that influence or impact their ability to manage stress.

While stress is a normal response when exposed to difficult situation, a person's stress response may also be conceptualised differently through the trauma-informed lens. While trauma is a huge predisposing factor on its own in relation to stress response (discussed as a sub-theme in Chapter 9) and there are several ways to explore the person's ability to manage stress, the following is only highlighted as a reference point for the therapist.

American Counselling Association (2023) outlined the following predisposing factors related to coping with disasters and trauma:

- Exposure to war
- Terrorism
- Violence and aggression
- Poor coping abilities and strategies
- Difficulty learning from previous experiences
- Low self-esteem
- Unstable work history

- Lack of finances
- Chemical dependency
- Chronic mental health issues (e.g., obsessive-compulsive disorders, anxiety disorders, Post Traumatic Stress Disorder (PTSD), depression, etc.)
- Past and/or present legal problems.
- Impulsivity,
- All-or-nothing thinking
- Negative perception of other people's responses
- Negative perceptions of symptoms
- Exaggeration of future probability of a critical incident
- Catastrophic attribution of responsibility
- Family transitions (e.g., marriage, divorce, death, birth of a child, child leaving home, etc.)
- Work stress (e.g., work hours, unreasonable expectations, lack of resources, etc.)
- Previous critical incidents in a short time frame

Hence, when exploring interpersonal relationships using this sub-theme, it is important to highlight to the person that the capacity and ability to tolerate distress and manage stress are further impacted by previous experiences, but also becoming a mother/father/parent itself impacts the person's capacity and ability to manage stress.

j. Sexual/intimacy (dis)satisfaction

Sexuality is a multidimensional phenomenon that makes up one of the most complex parts of human life. However, not every therapist or therapeutic relationships will address sexuality in the sessions for a number of reasons. Sexuality is not an easy topic to discuss or explore for all. Yet satisfaction or dissatisfaction arising from this area can have significant ripple effect on the person's overall well-being and impact multiple aspects of their life. Sexual function is impacted by several factors such as hormonal activity, menstruation, stage of life, age, psychological and emotional well-being, pregnancy, childbirth, breastfeeding, menopause to name a few. Women experience several significant changes in the perinatal period such as physical, hormonal, emotional and other. All of these changes have the potential to impact sexual function a great deal. This sub-theme is a reminder for the therapist to consider the importance of sexuality in human life and the significance of discussing this area, especially within the perinatal period with their clients.

Research in this area is ongoing, and the results are reflective of the time we live in. For the purposes of this discussion, the following is a brief overview of a recent meta-analysis conducted in this area. Grussu et al. (2021) divided their findings into two major categories: (1) **Sexual health during pregnancy** and (2) **sexual health during postnatal period**.

1 **Sexual health during pregnancy**: Grussu et al. (2021) highlighted that penetrative sex gradually declines during pregnancy. Especially from the second

trimester usually the decline begins, and a sharp decline tends to commence from the third trimester. The preference for the type of intercourse or the vaginal penetrative position tends to vary during each trimester according to the results of the meta-analysis (Grussu et al., 2021). However, they also noticed that couples who are more intimate than others tend to engage in negotiations and open communication about sexual positions that are comfortable and desirable for all involved. Grussu et al. (2021) also found mixed results when it came to the frequency of vaginal penetrative sexual activities, other non-coital activities such as anal, oral and masturbation, and other non-genital tenderness and stimulation among couples during pregnancy. Furthermore, the third trimester seems to be the time when most women will find a general decline in the frequency and occurrences of orgasm, desire and overall enjoyment from sexual relations. Grussu et al.'s (2021, p. 3) meta-analysis described this as a general "deterioration in desire, orgasm, lubrication, satisfaction, and pain in the third trimester". Grussu et al. (2021, p. 3) further found the following physical factors to be mostly accounting for these changes.

> Reduced frequency of sexual relations and a preference for different sexual positions are linked to fatigue, back pain, dyspareunia, infections and vulvar varicose veins…and changes in body shape…that diminish a woman's sense of security with respect to her own body. The orgasmic response is reduced due to a decrease of the connective vaginal tissue and a thickening of the muscle fibres of the vaginal cavity in anticipation of childbirth, while vaginal vasocongestion with reduced lubrication appears to increase pain during intercourse… Changes on a hormonal level during the period of pregnancy have an impact without having a significant influence on sexuality…Higher levels of estrogen, progesterone and prolactin can cause nausea, fatigue, and weight gain that can lead to a diminished desire and capacity for sexual arousal…

Dyspareunia is a medical term for painful sexual intercourse, a complex disorder that often is neglected, left undiagnosed and yet remains highly relevant within the perinatal period. Barret et al. (2000) confirmed that in most counselling sessions or medical appointments where sexual function and activities are discussed between perinatal patients and practitioners, the conversation tends to be about suitable birth control options and the timeline for the resumption of sexual activities. Despite an estimated 17–36% of women experiencing dyspareunia during the first six months postpartum both the patients and their healthcare providers in most cases fail to talk about this (Alligood-Percoco et al., 2016). "Dyspareunia and vaginismus are the two most common sexual dysfunctions in women" according to Sadovsky (2000). Both are highly relevant to the perinatal period, and both involve pain in relation to sexual activities; however, they are different and should be discussed with medical professionals. In relation to perinatal counselling, it is important that the therapist provides a safe, open and inviting space for the person to be able to describe and address pain and dissatisfaction in relation to sexual intimacy. For the purpose of this sub-theme, Sadovsky's (2000) following comment on the differences between the two conditions is provided below.

> Dyspareunia is recurrent genital pain caused by sexual activity. Primary dyspareunia is defined as constant pain during sexual activity, while secondary dyspareunia occurs after a period of pain-free lovemaking. Vaginismus is a conditioned pain caused by involuntary spasm of the muscles around the lower one third of the vagina, resulting from the association of sexual activity with pain and fear.

Grussu et al. (2021, p. 3) noted further psychological factors that usually contribute to the decline of a couple's sexual health in the following way.

> Anxiety relative to childbirth and to the new maternal role, the transformation of the couple relationship, and any experiences related to an earlier miscarriage all impact sexuality in pregnancy [15]. Awareness of a changed body image, the perception of a loss of attractiveness and lower self-esteem, accentuated in the third trimester of pregnancy, can lead to a decrease in sexual interest and activity [12,13,15]. Conversely, some women can perceive themselves to be more attractive and in sync with their own body due to breast enlargement or because they experience pregnancy as a time of positive contact with oneself and with the world.

Grussu et al.'s (2021, p. 3) meta-analysis further clarified that the couple or the female-bodied partner's fears about the following areas may also affect their sexual health during pregnancy such as injury to the foetus, damaging the placenta, having infection, premature birth and diverse cultural and religious beliefs about sex.

2 **Sexual health in the postnatal period**: Grussu et al.'s (2021) meta-analysis highlighted that most couples tend to resume their sexual behaviour six to eight weeks postpartum, whereas a steady and gradual recovery of sexual health occurs around or after six months postpartum. However, in most relationships, the sexual health of the people involved do not return to the pre-pregnancy level (Grussu et al., 2021, p. 6).

> Compared to the pre-pregnancy level, six months after childbirth, the frequency of any kind of sexual behaviour, be it coital or noncoital, is reduced... and this difference is evident for the entire first year of the child's life in the majority of couples... The resumption of noncoital sexual contact typically occurs before vaginal sexual intercourse... Oral sex and masturbation are the practices reported by couples in the first four weeks. Furthermore, masturbation is the first noncoital behaviour to return to pre-pregnancy frequency levels...

The factors that usually contribute to sexual health and function during the perinatal period are as follows: Perineal pain, dyspareunia, diminished desire to have sexual intimacy, assisted vaginal birth, damage to the pudendal nerve and anal sphincter during the birthing process, other physical damages from vaginal birth, complications from c-section, hormonal changes and heightened nipple sensitivity associated to breastfeeding and postnatal depression and/or other mental health difficulties. It is important to note that the existing research would show mixed results on the impact of breastfeeding on sexual health in the postnatal period. Below is a snapshot from Grussu et al.'s meta-analytic study capturing the mixed result (2021, p. 6).

> Breastfeeding can positively influence sexuality due to larger breast size and greater sensitivity of the nipples that can lead to a perception of better body image, heightened erotic response to breast stimulation, and greater desire… the release of oxytocin during breastfeeding can lead to sexual arousal and the characterization of breastfeeding as an erotic experience…the negative effects of breastfeeding on sexuality that appear to be more relevant, such as lower frequency of sexual activity, less interest in sex, diminished pleasure, decreased desire, and dyspareunia…breastfeeding that seems to have an impact on sexuality, but rather its duration. Women who breastfeed longer resume sexual activity later, have less interest in sex, and experience more pain and less pleasure during sexual intercourse…the impact of breastfeeding is quite different for women who breastfeed exclusively, compared to those who combine breastfeeding with bottle-feeding (of breast milk and/or formula), and those who bottle feed solely formula. These differences influence the parent's amount of sleep and fatigue which can affect the decision whether or not to engage in sexual intercourse.

k. Decision on finances

This sub-theme aims to provide the therapist with an opportunity to open up a dialogue about the person's financial situation and how it may to may not be impacting their mental health. Finance is another sensitive issue such as intimacy and sex that not everyone is comfortable about discussing. It is a topic that requires trust and openness from all involved in the relationship to be discussed and managed respectfully. The person becoming a mother/father/parent may or may not be financially independent during their perinatal period. However, their mental health within the perinatal period is dependent on their partner's support, which includes finance. Antoniou et al. (2021) highlighted the following in their systematic review of perinatal mental health examining the role and the effect of partner.

> partner support was a major predictor for maternal distress. A poor-quality couple relationship, particularly in conjunction with other stressors such as financial difficulties, partner infidelity, partner tension and domestic violence, is a strong predictor for perinatal distress.

As stated above, financial problems are one of the major factors that can contribute to perinatal mental health and well-being. However, decisions on finance are not always openly discussed and planned by the couple or the people involved in rearing the child during the perinatal period. Usually, the arrival of the new baby brings in a certain amount of financial burden to most families, even when the pregnancy was planned. A couple's decisions regarding their finance are never so important and require to be discussed more openly than in the perinatal period. Usually, there are four major ways that couples tend to operate financially:

1   Keeping each other's money in separate bank accounts and paying all bills equally from their own accounts
2   Keeping each other's money in separate bank accounts, paying some bills from their own accounts depending on their decision and division of bills such as one pays for electricity and grocery and the other(s) pays for rent or mortgage, etc
3   Paying all bills from a single joint account where all the incoming money gets deposited such as wages for the couple or the persons involved
4   One person brings wages in and pays weekly or monthly allowances to partner as per discussion

It depends on the couple or the household as to what works best for them. However, it is imperative that an open discussion takes place between all involved. Reminding the client of this fact is very useful. Some of the most difficult talks among parents might be the discussion around and decisions about not returning to their previous employment or deciding to be a full-time carer as for some people it makes more financial sense to do so. The financial dependency in this case on the partner and its psychological impact are complex and significant. Especially, the partner who stays at home and cares for the new child might find themselves in a vulnerable spot and requires partner support including open communication about finances and their impact. It becomes much more difficult and vulnerable for fathers or male partners if they decide to stay home and become full-time carer. This is because we have created a society where "care" has become synonymous to "females" and "masculinity" has become a narrow and toxic concept that torments any of us who dares to be decent, kind and anything different than the mythical categories of "man" or "woman" that we have created as a human race.

I. Conflicts about child rearing

Parental conflict has lasting impact on the children and the parents. Barnardo's (2023) highlighted that children can have lasting impacts on them when they,

> …witness adults who shout loudly, argue a lot or perhaps ignore one another frequently or for long periods of time, it can have a negative impact on children's self-esteem, mental and physical health, behaviour and academic achievements and future relationships with others.

This sub-theme is aimed at addressing the overall topic of parental conflict and allow the person to have an open discussion with the therapist about their experience at home. There are several ways to explore this topic in a therapeutic setting. The following are snippets from major resources that provide a baseline for the therapist when exploring this sub-theme.

According to the gov.uk (2021), parental conflict is a phenomenon that is to be conceptualised as situated just under the threshold of domestic abuse.

> Some level of arguing and conflict between parents is often a normal part of everyday life. However, there is strong evidence to show how inter-parental conflict that is frequent, intense and poorly resolved can have a significant negative impact on children's mental health and long-term life chances.

The UK Government further clarified on their website the following about parental conflict (gov.uk, 2021):

Damaging conflict (below this threshold) between parents can be expressed in many ways such as:

- Aggression
- Silence
- Lack of respect
- Lack of resolution

Conflict can affect children in all types of parental relationships, including:

- Parents who are in a relationship, whether married or not
- Parents who have separated or divorced
- Biological and step parents
- Other family members playing a parenting role
- Foster and adoptive parents
- Same-sex couples

All conflicts "can vary in nature, intensity and impact" according to The Children and Family Court Advisory and Support Service (CAFCASS) in the UK (CAFCASS 2017). However, they recognise "harmful conflict as conflict of any level which is detrimental to the child's wellbeing" (CAFCASS 2017). They highlighted the following behaviours or features "as being indicative of harmful conflict between parties: a high degree of anger or mistrust; verbal abuse; ongoing difficulties in communication and cooperation; loss of focus on the child; lengthy proceedings or repeat litigation" (CAFCASS 2017). CAFCASS (2017) highlighted three types of harmful conflicts.

Low-level conflict is generally issue-focused. While the parents may have clear differences or preferences, they are often able to negotiate a solution to the conflict

Medium-level conflict typically includes greater levels of blaming and may include patterns of relating carried over from experiences in their own family

High-level conflict is defined by Weeks and Treat (2001) as having a "chronic quality", and a "high degree of emotional reactivity, blaming and vilification". The distinctive feature is the refusal to submit to one another's rules, requests, or demands (Johnstone & Dallos, 2006).

Bernardo's (2023) identified the following common factors that lead to parental conflicts: Differences in parenting styles, having a new baby, financial concerns, housing-related difficulties (such as lack of own space), health reacted difficulties (such as illness), substance or alcohol misuse or other addiction.

The American Academy of Paediatrics (HealthyChildren.org, 2004) highlighted the following factors as contributing to parental conflict: **Inconsistency** – e.g., differences in rules and expectations for the child or undermining the authority of the other parent; **Non-communication** – e.g., staying silent or avoiding talking about issues or difficulties or differences; **Confusion** – e.g., not knowing how much supervision required or how much leniency needed or what is expected or how to react appropriately; **Competition** – e.g., rivalry between parents for a number reasons such as child's attention or love, unhealthy point scoring opportunity among the couple for their own fights and arguments using children; **Overt Conflict** – the Academy of Paediatrics (HealthyChildren.org, 2004) highlighted this factor in the following way.

> Too often, parents argue and openly challenge each other on family-related matters. Perhaps their child has gotten into trouble at school, and the parents disagree about how to handle it; the mother may think the child should be grounded, while the father believes it wasn't her fault. They start to argue - sometimes for hours or even over a period of days - and eventually, rather than resolving the problem amicably, one parent wins out because the other ultimately gives in, at least for the moment. Nevertheless, the parental power struggle often begins all over again at a later time with a different issue, with some of the same anger from the previous conflict resurfacing. The wounds never fully heal and the animosity builds.

m. Family history of distress (including trauma)

Family stress or distress can be defined in several ways. This sub-theme aims to explore this topic with the person from family unit perspective, rather than individual factors and their impact. In that sense, this theme seeks to explore the dynamics of the family unit due to stressors or factors that impacted the family as a whole including past trauma in the family. The following section will highlight some of the most relevant available literature for the therapist's considerations.

The Encyclopaedia of Quality of Life and Well-Being Research defines family stress as below (Boss, 2014).

> Family stress is defined as disturbance in the steady state of the family system. The disturbance can emerge from the outside context (e.g., war, unemployment),

from inside the family (e.g., death; divorce), or both simultaneously. In any case, the family system's equilibrium is threatened or disturbed. Family stress is therefore also defined as change in the family's equilibrium. Such change can be expected (as with the birth of a baby) or unexpected (as with winning a lottery).

Within the field of parenting, family or parent-child relationship, there is ample amount of literature available that identifies major stressors for family. Most of them refer to these broad four categories as the main stressors for a family: Marital dissatisfaction, home chaos, parental depressive symptoms and job role dissatisfaction (Nelson et al., 2009).

Evolutionary anthropologist Dewar (2023) highlighted the following two major causes for family stress: (1) Stressors originated from outside – such as job-related issues, job loss, racial discrimination, financial difficulties, neighbourhood or living situation-related issues such as crime, noise, pollution, poverty and similar. (2) Stressors originated from within the family – such as postnatal depression or anxiety, infant behaviour such as excessive crying, marital dissatisfaction, arguments, divorce, separation, difficult co-parenting, legal proceedings, interpersonal difficulties among family members such as sibling fights or adult children and parent relationship difficulties, death or imprisonment of family member, illness (physical and mental), sleep-related issues such as exhaustion and "perceptions of household chaos (which includes feelings of commotion, being rushed, running late all the time, having trouble staying on top of things, not being able to hear yourself think)" (Dewar, 2023).

Furthermore, in a recent study, Slopen et al. (2022) highlighted several major stressors that they identified as social determinants of health among caregivers and young children from age 0–5 years old.

1 Perceived stress in the past 12 months
2 Major life events

   • Death of an offspring
   • Experience of serious personal attack or assault
   • Witnessing serious physical attack or assault
   • Illness or accident such as near-death experience
   • Near-death experience of spouse or child from illness or accident

3 Everyday discrimination

   • Treated with less courtesy and respect than others
   • Receive poor service than others in restaurant and stores
   • Being treated by others as if not smart
   • Being treated as people need to be afraid of
   • Being threatened and harassed

4 Housing instability

   • Moved houses during and post pregnancy (number of times)

5 Job instability

- Moved jobs during and post pregnancy (number of times)

6 Work schedule instability

- Not knowing work schedule (hours) in advance week to week

7 Job insecurity

- Probability of losing main employment in the next couple of years

8 Work–life balance stress

- Job leaves one feeling too tired or stressed to participate in home or social activities after work

9 Financial insecurity

- Family finances not working well at the end of the month

10 Negative religious coping

- Belief after stressful event that God is punishing one for lack of faith/ spirituality
- Belief after stressful event that God has abandoned one

11 Neighborhood safety

- Feeling of safety walking around neighbourhood alone after dark (self and/ or child)

12 Family immigration concerns

- Worried about immigration-related issues for self or others

13 Stressful events 12 months prior to conception of the child attending the clinic
14 Stressful events during pregnancy
15 Stressful events since the child was born
16 Adverse childhood experiences of the respondent (reflecting on experience before age 18)

The abovementioned information is intended to provide the therapist with an opportunity to engage with the most relevant literature relevant to this sub-theme at a place in this chapter. It is not intended to be used as a comprehensive pickier of this field. The intention is to help the therapist be aware of the importance of this topic and the major contributing factors when working with perinatal clients making sense of the distress they present in the counselling sessions.

Conclusion

This chapter explored one of the ten major themes of the Becoming model: Couple relationship and/or co-parenting relationship and its related thirteen sub-themes.

The central aim of this chapter was to highlight that a number of factors that are part of the relationship and dynamics between the couple/parent have the potential to contribute to perinatal distress. The chapter also provided snippets from some of the latest research and/or reputable sources relevant to the sub-themes as a starting point for therapists' consideration. The next chapter will explore the major theme "Experiences of being parented".

References

Alligood-Percoco, N. R., Kjerulff, K. H., & Repke, J. T. (2016). Risk factors for dyspareunia after first childbirth. *Obstetrics and Gynecology, 128*(3), 512–518.

American Counselling Association. (2023). Retrieved from https://www.counseling.org/docs/trauma-disaster/fact-sheet-8---personal-and-pre-disposing-factors.pdf?sfvrsn=3629e0b7_2

Antoniou, E., Stamoulou, P., Tzanoulinou, M. D., & Orovou, E. (2021). Perinatal mental health; the role and the effect of the partner: A systematic review. *Healthcare (Basel, Switzerland), 9*(11), 1572. https://doi.org/10.3390/healthcare9111572

APA. (2023). *American Psychological Association dictionary of psychology* (online). Retrieved from https://dictionary.apa.org

Barrett, G., Pendry, E., Peacock, J., Victor, C., Thakar, R., & Manyonda, I. (2000). Women's sexual health after childbirth. *British Journal of Obstetrics and Gynecology, 107*(2), 186–95.

Baumrind, D. (1971). Current patterns of parental authority. *Developmental Psychology, 4*(1, Pt.2), 1–103. https://doi.org/10.1037/h0030372

Baumrind, D. (1991). The influence of parenting style on adolescent competence and substance use. *The Journal of Early Adolescence, 11*(1), 56–95. https://doi.org/10.1177/0272431691111004

Bernardo's (2023). *Parental conflict.* Retrieved from https://families.barnardos.org.uk/families/parental-conflicts

Bitter, J. R. (1993). Communication styles, personality priorities, and social interest: Strategies for helping couples build a life together. *Individual Psychology, 49*(3), 330. Retrieved from https://www.proquest.com/scholarly-journals/communication-styles-personality-priorities/docview/1303450403/se-2

Boss, P. (2014). Family stress. In A. C. Michalos (Ed.), *Encyclopedia of quality of life and well-being research.* Springer.

Bourne, J. E. (1995). *The anxiety and phobia workbook* (2nd ed.). New Harbinger Publications, Inc.

CAFCASS. (2017). *Harmful conflict.* Retrieved from https://www.cafcass.gov.uk/parent-carer-or-family-member/applications-child-arrangements-order/how-your-family-court-adviser-makes-their-assessment-your-childs-welfare-and-best-interests/harmful-conflict

Dewar. (2023). *Family stress: An evidence based guide.* ParentingScience.com. Retrieved from https://parentingscience.com/family-stress/

gov.uk (2021). *Guidance: Reducing parental conflict: What is parental conflict?* Retrieved from https://www.gov.uk/guidance/reducing-parental-conflict-what-is-parental-conflict

Grussu, P., Vicini, B., & Quatraro, R. M. (2021). Sexuality in the perinatal period: A systematic review of reviews and recommendations for Practice. *Sexual & Reproductive Healthcare, 30*, 100668. https://doi.org/10.1016/j.srhc.2021.100668

HealthyChildren.org (2004). Parenting conflicts. *American Academy of Paediatrics*. Retrieved from https://www.healthychildren.org/English/family-life/family-dynamics/Pages/Parenting-Conflicts.aspx

Johnstone, L., & Dallos, R. (Eds.). (2006). *Formulation in psychology and psychotherapy: Making sense of people's problems*. Routledge.

Kefir, N. (1971). *Priorities: A different approach to lifestyle and neurosis* [Paper presentation]. ICASSI.

Maccoby, E. E., & Martin, J. A. (1983). Socialization in the Context of the Family: Parent-Child Interaction. In P. H. Mussen, & E. M. Hetherington (Eds.), *Handbook of child psychology: Vol. 4. Socialization, Personality, and Social Development* (pp. 1–101). Wiley.

Nelson, J. A., O'Brien, M., Blankson, A. N., Calkins, S. D., & Keane, S. P. (2009). Family stress and parental responses to children's negative emotions: Tests of the spillover, cross-over, and compensatory hypotheses. *Journal of Family Psychology: JFP: Journal of the Division of Family Psychology of the American Psychological Association (Division 43)*, *23*(5), 671–679. https://doi.org/10.1037/a0015977

Parker G. (2007). Is depression overdiagnosed? Yes. *BMJ (Clinical research ed.)*, *335*(7615), 328. https://doi.org/10.1136/bmj.39268.475799.AD

Satir, V. (1976). *Making contact*. Celestial Arts.

Sadovsky, R. (2000). Management of dyspareunia and vaginismus. *American Family Physician*, *61*(8), 2511–2512.

Slopen, N., Cook, B. L., Morgan, J. W., Flores, M. W., Mateo, C., Coll, C. G., Garcia, D. A., Priest, N., Wethington, E., Lee, E., Moyer, M., Tran, N. M., Krumholz, S., & Williams, D. R. (2022). Family stressors and resources as social determinants of health among caregivers and young children. *Children*, *9*(4), 452. https://doi.org/10.3390/children9040452

Weeks, G.R., & Treat, S. (2001) *Couples in treatment: Techniques and approaches for effective practice* (2nd ed.). Brunner/Routledge.

Chapter 9

Experiences of Being Parented

Sub-themes:

a Dynamics between parents/caregivers
b Trauma, estrangement, ACE
c Current involvement or lack of
d Parents/caregivers' parenting style

Introduction

This chapter explores the major theme "Experiences of being parented" and its four sub-themes. The chapter highlights the central role that this theme and the sub-themes play in the manifestation of most difficulties and psychological discomforts experienced in the perinatal period despite having a seemingly healthy childhood and without any Adverse Childhood Experience (ACE). The main aim of this chapter is to highlight that one's experiences of being parented can influence and has the potential to impact one's experience of becoming a parent even without any sign of trauma or ACE in their own life. This is done by including snippets from recent research literature as baseline information on these topics that the therapist can use as starting the discussion with their clients.

a. Dynamics between parents/caregivers

This sub-theme aims to explore the person's perception of their parents' or caregivers' interpersonal relationship, particularly focusing on parent-parent relationship, its impact on the person as their child and its impact on the person as someone who is now becoming a parent themselves. There are several ways the therapist can explore this sub-theme depending on their training and the context of the session. However, the following is a snapshot of the major dimensions of this sub-theme captured in a recent study.

van Eldik et al. (2020) highlighted six major dimensions of inter-parental relationship in their research based on major theoretical frameworks:

- Relationship quality
- Conflict frequency
- Hostile
- Disengaged and un-constructive forms of conflict
- Child-related conflict.

They further highlighted that children can develop maladjusted symptoms in relation to inter-parental relationship and they can be both and/or externalising

DOI: 10.4324/9781003309710-10

symptoms and internalising symptoms (van Eldik et al., 2020). Children's overall responses to inter-parental relationship can also be several types such as emotional, behavioral, cognitive and physiological (van Eldik et al., 2020). Their results were further supported by the findings from the Early Intervention Foundation's research conducted by the British Government (Harold et al., 2016) highlighted below.

> …the quality of the inter-parental relationship, specifically how parents communicate and relate to each other, is increasingly recognised as a primary influence on effective parenting practices and children's long-term mental health and future life chances
>
> Children of all ages can be affected by destructive inter-parental conflict, with effects evidenced across infancy, childhood, adolescence, and adulthood.
>
> Inter-parental conflict can adversely affect both the mother–child and father–child relationships, with evidence suggesting that the association between inter-parental conflict and negative parenting practices may be stronger for the father–child relationship compared to the mother–child relationship.

Interparental relationship is significant in considering children's wellbeing. Therapists interested in learning about programmes that aim to enhance the interparental relationship and improve outcomes for children see Gordon et al. (2018). The above are the most relevant findings to consider when working with this sub-theme. Especially these findings are worth considering when the therapist is trying to understand the perinatal client's experience and their partner or significant other's experience as children being parented by their parents in past. The experience of being parented and witnessing inter-parental conflicts or other dimensions mentioned above will have an impact on the perinatal client and their partner(s)' position as a parent themselves.

b. Trauma, estrangement, ACE

This sub-theme aims to explore the aspects of the person's experiences of being parented that may have been traumatic, may have involved estrangement and perhaps ACEs. One of the major predisposing factors for stress and mental health difficulties is ACE, an acronym for Adverse Childhood Experience. According to the Centres for Disease Control and Prevention (CDC) "ACE's are potentially traumatic events that occur in childhood (0-17 years)" (CDC, 2022). The Centre on the Developing Child at Harvard University highlighted the following two points about ACE (Harvard University, 2023):

1 ACEs are quite common, even among a middle-class population: More than two-thirds of the population report experiencing one ACE, and nearly a quarter have experienced three or more
2 There is a powerful, persistent correlation between the more ACEs experienced and the greater the chance of poor outcomes later in life, including dramatically

increased risk of heart disease, diabetes, obesity, depression, substance abuse, smoking, poor academic achievement, time out of work and early death

The CDC outlined the following factors that increase the likelihood of someone experiencing ACEs before the age of 17 (CDC, 2021):

- Families experiencing caregiving challenges related to children with special needs (e.g., disabilities, mental health issues and chronic physical illnesses)
- Children and youth who don't feel close to their parents/caregivers and feel like they can't talk to them about their feelings
- Youth who start dating early or engaging in sexual activity early
- Children and youth with few or no friends or with friends who engage in aggressive or delinquent behaviour
- Families with caregivers who have a limited understanding of children's needs or development
- Families with caregivers who were abused or neglected as children
- Families with young caregivers or single parents
- Families with low income
- Families with adults with low levels of education
- Families experiencing high levels of parenting stress or economic stress
- Families with caregivers who use spanking and other forms of corporal punishment for discipline
- Families with inconsistent discipline and/or low levels of parental monitoring and supervision
- Families that are isolated from and not connected to other people (extended family, friends, neighbours)
- Families with high conflict and negative communication styles
- Families with attitudes accepting of or justifying violence or aggression

It is important to highlight that "Estrangement" can be one of the ACEs and the experience of parental or sibling estrangement may add further complexity to the person's journey through motherhood and fatherhood. The American Psychiatric Association (APA) dictionary described estrangement as: (1) "a state of increased distance or separation from oneself or others", and (2) "a significant decrease or discontinuation of contact with individuals with whom one formerly had close relationships, such as a spouse or family member, due to apathy or antagonism" (APA, 2023). There is no consensus on the definition of estrangement among researchers, but overall, "Relationships between adult family members that are distant or inactive are increasingly referred to as 'estranged'" (Blake et al., 2022). Estrangement is also considered "as a healthy response to an unhealthy situation" (Blake et al., 2022).

Adult children and parents who are estranged from one another can experience "feeling sad, shocked, angry and disappointed" (Blake et al., 2022). However, adult children can also experience "loss of the emotional, financial and practical support that family members can provide to one another" (ibid). Adult children who are estranged from their parents and are becoming a parent themselves would often experience guilt and/or shame for a number of reasons. Especially they may try to keep this (estrangement) aspect of their life private as they fear that they may not be "normal". Their experience of being parented may have also left them with questions about themselves and their own ability to parent, irrespective of reality. Not to mention that there may be an accompanied felt sense of lack of support and/or social isolation as their offspring have no connection with their grandparents or other significant family members due to estrangement. Hence, estrangement may cause ripple effect in several aspects of a parent's life, may negatively impact their interpersonal relationships and in some cases lead to a sense of social isolation (Blake et al., 2022). Estrangement from previous children while parenting new children may also bring further complexities in the psyche of the parent(s). For instance, a father or a mother who is no longer in touch with their child or children for a number of reasons, such as misunderstandings or other felt sense of betrayal or similar, might experience guilt, shame, grief or other complex emotions while becoming a parent again in a new relationship. Some contributing factors that may lead to estrangement overlap with ACEs. The following quote captures some of these factors as they all contribute to some form of family distress (Blake et al., 2022).

> …children experiencing sexual, physical, and/or psychological abuse and/or neglect; poor parenting and feelings of betrayal; drug abuse, changing family forms, disagreements, romantic relationships, politics, homophobia, and issues relating to money, inheritance, or business…Family estrangement may also be initiated or exacerbated by physical and/or mental health problems in the family.

The Centre on the Developing Child at Harvard University highlighted the connection between trauma and ACE in the following way (Harvard University, 2023).

> While trauma has many definitions, typically in psychology it refers to an experience of serious adversity or terror—or the emotional or psychological *response* to that experience. **Trauma-informed care** or services are characterized by an understanding that problematic behaviors may need to be treated as a result of the ACEs or other traumatic experiences someone has had, as opposed to addressing them as simply willful and/or punishable actions.

Considering the complexities of the field of trauma-informed care, this discussion will only highlight the need for the therapist to be addressing or be open to addressing this sub-theme and consider the overlaps between previous experiences of the person being parented as a child and their experience of parenting as an adult now. The definition of trauma used in this sub-theme for the purpose of the clinician beginning a discussion with their clients is based on the entry in the APA dictionary (APA, 2023).

> …any disturbing experience that results in significant fear, helplessness, dissociation, confusion, or other disruptive feelings intense enough to have a

long-lasting negative effect on a person's attitudes, behavior, and other aspects of functioning. Traumatic events include those caused by human behavior (e.g., rape, war, industrial accidents) as well as by nature (e.g., earthquakes) and often challenge an individual's view of the world as a just, safe, and predictable place.

c. Current involvement or lack of

This sub-theme aims to explore the current level of involvement of the grandparents of the person or the level of involvement of those who are parental figures to the person or were caregivers to the person when they were children. The level of involvement will probably depend on a number of factors related to the history of the parents being parented. Grandparents can be involved for a number of reasons and in a number of ways such as custodial, residential and non-residential and others. Each of these involvements comes with its own sets of complexities such as roles, expectations and boundaries.

Grandparents can also not be involved for a number of reasons such as illness or disabilities, absent by choice, absent due to previous history of misunderstanding or estrangement, absent due to geographical barriers such as immigration, financial hardship or other issues. Each family is different and unique. Moreover, each person is unique in their individuality and their experience of being parented is also unique. Even if they are reared in the same family, each sibling may have different experiences of being parented by the same parents.

Furthermore, each grandparent will have their own unique ways of navigating the role of grandparenting. In that sense, they too are "becoming grand-parent", a phenomenon that is in the making and is equally if not *more* complex than the journey that their children undertake of "becoming a parent". Considering these unique factors and the complexities involved, this sub-theme is a reminder for the clinician to open up a dialogue with the client to explore their experiences of their parents and/or their partner's parents involvement or the lack of it in their and their children's lives.

d. Parents/caregivers' parenting style

This sub-theme aims to explore the parenting style witnessed and experienced by the parents of their parents, and the impact such experience may have on the parents' journey of "becoming a mother/father". Parenting style has been described in Chapter 8 as a sub-theme from the perspective of co-parenting. This sub-theme explores the parenting style of the grandparents as witnessed by the parents. In this regard, it is important to note that when a person is recalling their experiences of being parented, it is useful to consider such account as "remembered" or "perceived" parenting style, rather than "actual" parenting style. This is the language that most researchers use to capture and study the field of the impacts on adulthood of their remembered parenting style.

For example, Rothrauff et al. (2009) concluded in their research that how a person remembers their parent's parenting style or their parents' behaviour will have an impact on the functioning of the person across their lifespan. While parental behaviour is multidimensional, parenting style mostly has two prominent elements: Support and control. Both are important for a child's emotional, physical and behavioural growth and development. However, inadequate proportion of either is associated with poor outcome of children's development and well-being in adulthood. For instance, Rothrauff et al. (2009) highlighted that parental support can predict "a strong sense of self-worth and security, greater psychological well-being, and other positive outcomes". However, the lack of adequate support may lead to children experiencing "anxiety, insecurity, aggression, hostility, low self-esteem, and inadequacy" (Rothrauff et al., 2009). Similarly, parental control can help children learn responsibility, conformity and self-control (ibid). Learning and abiding rules set by their parents, children get to understand the concept of consequences, develop problem-solving and decision-making skills and learn about societal standards (ibid). Parental control also teaches them self-control and self-regulation of emotions. However, too much or too little parental control can "make it difficult for children to manage effectively in the outside world where behavioral rules and standards of conduct exist in nearly all social settings" (Rothrauff et al., 2009). The purpose of this sub-theme has only been to help therapists understand the outcome of the remembered parenting style in adulthood as expressed by the client and its impact on their experience of "becoming a mother/father".

Conclusion

This chapter explored the major theme "Experiences of being parented" and its four sub-themes. The main aim was to highlight the central role that this theme and the sub-themes play in contributing to perinatal distress. The chapter also provided snippets from current literature to illustrate the importance of exploring one's experience of being parented during the perinatal period for the therapist's consideration. The next chapter will explore another major theme: Socio-economic background and its two sub-themes: Values, hopes, aspiration and gender-roles.

References

APA. (2023). *American Psychological Association dictionary of psychology* (online). Retrieved from https://dictionary.apa.org

Blake, L., Bland, B., & Gilbert, H. (2022). The efficacy of a facilitated support group intervention to reduce the psychological distress of individuals experiencing family estrangement, *Evaluation and Program Planning, 95.* Accessed from https://www.sciencedirect.com/science/article/pii/S0149718922001227

CDC. (2021). *Risk and protective factors.* Retrieved from https://www.cdc.gov/violenceprevention/aces/riskprotectivefactors.html

CDC. (2022). *Fast facts: Preventing adverse childhood experiences.* Retrieved from https://www.cdc.gov/violenceprevention/aces/fastfact.html

Gordon, H., Sellers, R., Chowdry, H., & Acquah, D. (2018, August 10). *What works to enhance interparental relationships and improve outcomes for children?* Retrieved March 28, 2023, from https://www.eif.org.uk/report/what-works-to-enhance-interparental-relationships-and-improve-outcomes-for-children

Harold, G., Acquah, D., Sellers, R and Chowdry, H. (2016) 'What works to enhance interparental relationships and improve outcomes for children?', Early Intervention Foundation. Available: https://www.eif.org.uk/report/what-works-to-enhance-interparental-relationships-and-improve-outcomes-for-children/. Accessed: 12/06/2019.

Harvard University. (2023). Retrieved from https://developingchild.harvard.edu/resources/aces-and-toxic-stress-frequently-asked-questions/

Rothrauff, T. C., Cooney, T. M., & An, J. S. (2009). Remembered parenting styles and adjustment in middle and late adulthood. *The Journals of Gerontology Series B: Psychological Sciences and Social Sciences, 64B*(1), 137–146. https://doi.org/10.1093/geronb/gbn008

van Eldik, W. M., de Haan, A. D., Parry, L. Q., Davies, P. T., Luijk, M. P. C. M., Arends, L. R., & Prinzie, P. (2020). The interparental relationship: Meta-analytic associations with children's maladjustment and responses to interparental conflict. *Psychological Bulletin, 146*(7), 553–594.

Chapter 10

Socio-economic Background

Sub-themes:

a Values, hopes, aspiration
b Gender roles

Introduction

This chapter will explore the major theme Socio-economic background and its related two sub-themes: Values, hopes, aspiration and Gender roles. The chapter will
explore the connection between socio-economic status (SES) and perinatal distress
or mental health difficulties in order to highlight the importance of exploring this
topic in perinatal counselling sessions. This is done by drawing for the field of
Marketing. A field that overlaps with social psychology.

Socio-economic status/background

There is already a wealth of knowledge widely available on the intersection of SES
and mental health in general for the therapist to be informed and to draw from. The
purpose of this theme here is to only highlight the importance of exploring this
topic with and its impact on the perinatal client in therapy. The American Psychological Association (APA, 2023) describes socio-economic status or background
referred to as SES in the following way.

> Socioeconomic status is the position of an individual or group on the socio-
> economic scale, which is determined by a combination of social and economic
> factors such as income, amount and kind of education, type and prestige of oc-
> cupation, place of residence, and—in some societies or parts of society—ethnic
> origin or religious background. Examinations of socioeconomic status often
> reveal inequities in access to resources, as well as issues related to privilege,
> power, and control.

SES is a term that captures a number of factors and is a highly relevant term both
within and outside the therapeutic setting.

> Socioeconomic status (SES) encompasses not just income but also educational
> attainment, financial security, and subjective perceptions of social status and so-
> cial class. Socioeconomic status can encompass quality of life attributes as well

DOI: 10.4324/9781003309710-11

as the opportunities and privileges afforded to people within society. Poverty, specifically, is not a single factor but rather is characterized by multiple physical and psychosocial stressors. Further, SES is a consistent and reliable predictor of a vast array of outcomes across the life span, including physical and psychological health. Thus, SES is relevant to all realms of behavioral and social science, including research, practice, education and advocacy.

Furthermore, distinctions between objective and subjective SES are highlighted below for the therapist's consideration. Objective SES is generally defined by the social dimension and refers to the person's access to material (Navarro-Carrillo et al., 2020).

This form of SES is usually operationalized by considering various objective indicators that may ultimately reflect differences in individuals' access to material and social resources. In particular, among the multiple objective indices of SES, three distinctive aspects emerge quite clearly: income, educational level, and occupation.

Access to material resources is not the only factor that helps conceptualise SES. One can determine their own socio-economic position by making subjective assessment, and in that sense, subjective SES is conceptualised based on individual's perception of themselves and described in the following way (Navarro-Carrillo et al., 2020).

…founded on social comparison processes (e.g., determining one's own socio-economic position relative to that of other individuals or groups)…Consistent with this emerging perspective, subjective SES is conceptualized as individuals' perceptions pertaining to their standing in the social hierarchy relative to others.

a. Values, hopes, aspiration

This sub-theme aims at exploring the person's values, hopes and aspiration and how they are shaped or impacted or influenced by the person's SES. There are several ways of exploring this sub-theme. One of the possible pathways to understand SES and its connection to psychology is to dive into cross-disciplinary research. Marketing seems to be an area that provides an insight into the intersection between SES and psychology. Values are central in determining one's actions and decisions. The field of Marketing has dedicated itself to understanding human values with a view to market products for the targeted population. The Association for consumer research highlighted the following (Beatty et al., 1988).

…values have a significant influence on, among other things, television viewing habits, activity preferences, store choice, consumer decision criteria, consumer product choice, reaction to discontinuous innovations, and cigarette smoking.

In 1978, Arnold Mitchell, a social scientist, developed a marketing research tool "determining the motivations behind consumer purchasing decisions" called Values, Attitudes and Lifestyles (VALS) for Socially Responsible Investment International (SRI International) founded by the Stanford University (SRI, 2022). The VALS framework identifies eight types of consumers based on their motivations. The APA dictionary has an entry on VALS as this is a concept that lies at the intersection of social psychology and Marketing. APA Dictionary described VALS as below (APA, 2023).

> a proprietary method of segmenting consumers according to their personal characteristics. Eight categories of consumers are identified on the basis of responses to proprietary questionnaires.

The categories are as follows: Achievers, Innovators, Thinkers, Believers, Strivers, Experiencers, Makers and Survivors. Strategic Business Insights (2020) clarified that VALS have two primary components: Primary motivation and resources. Strategic Business Insights (2020) noted the following.

> The concept of primary motivation explains consumer attitudes and anticipates behavior. VALS includes three primary motivations that matter for understanding consumer behavior: ideals, achievement, and self-expression. Consumers who are primarily motivated by ideals are guided by knowledge and principles. Consumers who are primarily motivated by achievement look for products and services that demonstrate success to their peers. Consumers who are primarily motivated by self-expression desire social or physical activity, variety, and risk. These motivations provide the necessary basis for communication with the VALS types and for a variety of strategic applications.

According to the abovementioned clarifications, Thinkers and Believers are motivated by ideals and they are guided by knowledge and principles. Strivers and Achievers are motivated by achievement and they seek "products and services that demonstrate success to their peers" (Strategic Business Insights, 2020). Makers and Experiencers are "primarily motivated by self-expression" and they "desire social or physical activity, variety, and risk". On the other hand, Strategic Business Insights (2020) clarified how the VALS framework to be understood from the resources perspective.

> A person's tendency to consume goods and services extends beyond age, income, and education. Energy, self-confidence, intellectualism, novelty seeking, innovativeness, impulsiveness, leadership, and vanity play a critical role. These psychological traits in conjunction with key demographics determine an individual's resources. Various levels of resources enhance or constrain a person's expression of his or her primary motivation

The combined categories of the VALS framework highlight a few aspects. (1) There is a strong connection between one's SES and motivation. In other words, the motivation to buy a particular packet of cereal is connected to one's SES. Similarly, one can argue that decisions that one makes in relation to their children will have a connection to their SES. For instance, the motivation to buy or not to buy particular products for the baby may have a connection to one's SES. If the other parent or partner is not from the SES, there may be differences in views and expectations. (2) There are also factors such as subjective perceptions of SES, subjective values and attitudes. These factors can also influence one's decisions, actions, hopes and aspiration. Meaning, how a person views their SES irrespective of what it really is will also influence their values, hopes and dreams, which in turn will influence one's decisions. For instance, what expectations one have about the child's future such as clothing style, schooling, types of books to read or not read, types of activities to engage in or not engage in will be influenced by the parent's values, which may be influenced by their SES. Once again, there may be differences in views among the parents or caregivers on these decisions as they may come from different SES or may subjectively assess their SES to be different from their partner. (3) There can be a massive difference in one's own subjective assessment of their SES and other's objective assessment of their SES based on information such as age, location, income, etc. Hence, it is quite possible that one may dream or hope for a certain future for their offspring that is not usually associated with their objective SES. Hence, it is beneficial to not pigeonhole a person due to their SES, not to be guided by statistical inferences, but rather consider the complexities of a human subject occupying unique spaces within the social and the economic world being influenced by their subjective values, hope and aspirations. In other words, not to assume but ask and explore how one's SES if at all influencing their decisions, dreams and hopes and also their relationship with their partners. Especially if there are differences in views and opinions at home, it is useful to understand how the client's views have been shaped by different factors including their SES if at all and whether they are aware of them. Above all, the therapist's clinical judgement must be exercised when exploring these topics.

b. Gender roles

This sub-theme aims to explore the aspect of the person that connects their gender and their SES. Gender is a societal construct, and hence gender roles are societal expectations that one usually becomes aware of very early on in their life and grows up with implications of these expectations in their psyche and in their choices. There are several ways that the therapist can explore this topic. The following are in no way comprehensive. They provide snippets of some significant literature that are relevant to this theme for the therapist's consideration to start a dialogue with their clients. The APA dictionary (APA, 2023) described gender as below.

1   The condition of being male, female or neuter. In a human context, the distinction between gender and sex reflects the usage of these terms: Sex usually refers to the biological aspects of maleness or femaleness, whereas gender implies the

psychological, behavioural, social and cultural aspects of being male or female (i.e., masculinity or femininity)

2   In linguistics, a grammatical category in inflected languages that governs the agreement between nouns and pronouns and adjectives

Furthermore, the APA Dictionary defined gender roles as below (APA, 2023).

the pattern of behavior, personality traits, and attitudes that define masculinity or femininity in a particular culture. It frequently is considered the external manifestation of the internalized gender identity, although the two are not necessarily consistent with one another.

This sub-theme also explores the biases related to their gender that the person has been exposed to as part of the social space that they occupy. The APA Dictionary defined gender bias as below (APA, 2023).

any one of a variety of stereotypical beliefs about individuals on the basis of their sex, particularly as related to the differential treatment of females and males. These biases often are expressed linguistically, as in use of the phrase physicians and their wives (instead of physicians and their spouses, which avoids the implication that physicians must be male) or of the term he when people of both sexes are being discussed.

This sub-theme is particularly important as the perinatal period is a time when one's body becomes much more important in the conversation than at other times. Especially the differences in bodies and the differences in gendered bodies become ever so prominent during the perinatal period. The societal expectations and biases that once were subtle and implicit may become explicit to the client during the perinatal period. The person becomes very aware of the societal expectations regarding what they ought to do or should behave like when they occupy a certain type of body with a certain set of genitalia and sexual organs. Such as the expectations of what a woman of a certain age should do, what a man from a certain neighbourhood should be like, what a mother from a certain class should teach their children or what a father from a certain economic background should have achieved by a certain age. The intersectionality of age, gender and SES is never so impactful than it is within the perinatal period. It is up to the therapist as to how they explore these themes and sub-themes. However, it is crucial that one's SES is taken into account as potential contributing factor for perinatal distress such as differences in views among partners leading to arguments and/or the internal struggle one may experience about their hopes and dreams for the new baby as they go against the popular views of people from their SES.

Conclusion

This chapter explored the major theme Socio-economic background and its related two sub-themes: Values, hopes, aspiration and gender roles. The chapter drew from the field of Marketing to illustrate how SES shapes one's values and dreams. It is crucial that the therapist invites the client to have a discussion and explores the connection between SES and their perinatal distress or mental health difficulties. The next chapter will explore the next major theme "History of previous diagnosis" and its two related sub-themes "Medical" and "Psychological".

References

APA. (2023). APA Dictionary of Psychology. Retrieved from https://dictionary.apa.org/

Beatty, S. E., Homer, P. M., & Kahle, L. R. (1988). Problems with VALS in international marketing research: An example from an application of the empirical mirror technique. In M. J. Houston (Ed.), *NA – advances in consumer research* (Vol. 15, pp. 375–380). Association for Consumer Research.

Navarro-Carrillo, G., Alonso-Ferres, M., Moya, M., & Valor-Segura, I. (2020, May 18). *Socioeconomic status and psychological well-being: Revisiting the role of subjective socioeconomic status.* Retrieved March 29, 2023, from https://www.frontiersin.org/articles/10.3389/fpsyg.2020.01303/full

SRI. (2022, June 29). *Vals™ market research.* Retrieved March 29, 2023, from https://www.sri.com/hoi/vals-market-research/

Strategic Business Insights. (2020). *Strategic business insights.* Retrieved March 29, 2023, from https://www.strategicbusinessinsights.com//vals/ustypes.shtml

Chapter 11

History of Previous Diagnosis

Sub-themes:

a Medical
b Psychological

Introduction

This chapter explores the major theme "History of previous diagnosis" and its two related sub-themes: Medical and Psychological. The chapter first addresses how different allied health professionals are trained to take history differently and emphasises on the crucial quality of empathy. The chapter then explores the sub-themes by drawing from some of the latest research literature on this topic. Finally, the chapter draws attention to the intersection of chronic conditions, its impact on caring, the experience of exhaustion and how they may impact one's well-being during the perinatal period.

This theme aims to explore the person's history of previous physical and mental health difficulties and diagnosis. Such history may also be referred to as medical history. Counselling clinic may not require taking a complete medical history in a similar manner that a medical practitioner's clinic would. It is still vital to address some aspects of the person's medical history when working with them therapeutically during the perinatal period in order to get a holistic picture of the person and the possible risk factors associated to their medical history. Part of this history-taking process is already done in the intake forms in most counselling settings. Allied health professionals such as psychologists, counsellors, psychotherapists and other clinicians who work in a therapeutic setting have their own training in history taking. All allied health professionals are trained in their unique ways to obtain a version of medical history that is relevant to their profession and their clients. This section is not aimed at replicating the therapist's own ways of obtaining this information. Rather the purpose of including this theme in the Becoming model is to highlight the importance of paying attention to the person's previous diagnosis and their medical, physical and psychological history as these factors may play a significant role in the person's sense of well-being during their perinatal period. Hence, in a therapeutic setting, it is not just about the forms or the formal way of knowing one's medical history. Rather it is about understanding the person's experience with those events and how (if at all) they might be impacting the person's life today, especially during their perinatal period. Such exploration and understanding require the therapist to create a non-judgmental, safe space for the person

DOI: 10.4324/9781003309710-12

and deepen therapeutic alliance. As Nichol et al. (2022) highlighted, it is not just about history taking, it is about communicating empathy and support.

> Obtaining a thorough history is important, but the questioning should show empathy to the patient and their condition...Patients may feel rushed or that the provider lacks empathy if questions are asked robotically.

a. Medical

Medical history "includes an inquiry into the patient's medical history, past surgical history, family medical history, social history, allergies, and medications the patient is taking or may have recently stopped taking" (Nichol et al., 2022). They further clarified the definition and purpose of medical history in the following way (Nichol et al., 2022).

> Obtaining a medical history can reveal the relevant chronic illnesses and other prior disease states for which the patient may not be under treatment but may have had lasting effects on the patient's health...In general, a medical history includes an inquiry into the patient's medical history, past surgical history, family medical history, social history, allergies, and medications the patient is taking or may have recently stopped taking.

Please note that the above may suggest that medical history does not involve psychiatric or psychological history. However, that is not the case. There are several overlaps between the two, and it is explained further in the next sub-theme below. Medical history focuses more on the physical aspect of the person, and from the perspective of the "Becoming model", the emphasis remains on understanding the presence or absence of risk factors from the person's past including genetic and environmental factors. In that sense, chronic illnesses and/or previous medical procedures that have left permanent damages or changes on the body and/or have significantly impacted the body's abilities and/or functioning are major risk factors to consider when working within the perinatal period.

The National Cancer Institute (NCI, 2023) defines chronic disease as "A disease or condition that usually lasts for 3 months or longer and may get worse over time...tend to occur in older adults and can usually be controlled but not cured". The Centre for Disease Control and Prevention (CDC, 2023) clarified that chronic conditions are much more prevalent than one might think, "Six in ten adults in the US have a chronic disease and four in ten adults have two or more".

The following are major examples of chronic disease: Heart disease, cancer, chronic lung disease, stroke, Alzheimer's, diabetes and chronic kidney disease. Research on chronic disease and its impact on parenting is mixed, and the following is only a snippet of a larger research field that is beyond the scope of this book to capture here. Kaasbøll et al. (2021), in their longitudinal study, highlighted the following mixed results on parental chronic illness and its impact on offspring's psychological health and well-being.

> A few studies have reported positive outcomes concerning parental chronic illness, strengthened interpersonal relationships and increased maturity among children…Many more studies have indicated that parental chronic illness increases the risk of reduced family functioning and social-emotional and behavioral problems in children and adolescents…The risk of adverse outcomes in offspring may increase with the duration and severity of the parent's illness.

The CDC (2023) outlined the following major risk factors for chronic disease: Tobacco use, poor nutrition, physical inactivity and excessive alcohol use. Consider the high prevalence of these factors in Western societies reflected in the following statistics. Globally 22.3% of the population used tobacco according to the WHO (2023a, 2023b, 2023c); globally 31–36% do not do enough physical activity to stay healthy according to the WHO (2023a, 2023b, 2023c), which is around 1 in 3 women and 1 in 4 men; over 26.2% of the global population, that is, 1.9 billion adults are overweight or obese, while 462 million are underweight according to the WHO (2023a, 2023b, 2023c); in 2021, approximately 55% of Irish adults (aged +18) reported to drink alcohol at least on a weekly basis (Drinkaware, 2023). The high prevalence of these risk factors indicate that it is very common to be living with a chronic disease and hence, it is important to explore the impact on the person who is becoming a parent, of the chronic conditions or the risk factors outlined above.

b. Psychological

One's psychological history includes their psychiatric history, family history and other developmental history. This is why psychological history is often referred to as psychiatric history.

> Acquiring a psychiatric history follows the same format as any medical history, with particular emphasis on developmental and social factors. It must also include the patient's past mental health history, including treatment and medications, and a history of family psychiatric disorders and treatment. (Wharff & Ginnis, 2007)

The method of psychological history taking varies widely as counsellors, psychotherapists, psychologists and other allied health professionals have their own training that is unique to their discipline to perform this task. This section does not aim to replicate this training. Rather this sub-theme is a reminder for the clinicians to explore and consider the psychological history of the person going through the perinatal period. Especially this sub-theme is included in the model to encourage the therapist to assess and address the pressure related to or arising from one's psychological history. This involves considering the risk factors that may exist in one's psychological history, that may elevate the person's stress level in the perinatal period and/or that may contribute to the onset of a previous condition.

The following quote is from the latest systematic review on the relapse and onset of serious mental health conditions during the perinatal period conducted by Taylor et al. (2019). They highlighted how common it is for women to have a relapse following birth if they had a previous history of serious mental health disorders in the following way (Taylor et al., 2019).

> Relapse of serious mental illness (psychotic and bipolar disorders) around childbirth is potentially devastating…The acute onset of psychoses immediately following childbirth are among the most severe disorders seen in psychiatry… women with bipolar disorder have high risk of relapse postpartum, with reported estimates ranging from 17 to 75%…Previous inpatient admissions, the number and recency of previous admissions and admission during pregnancy have been associated with postpartum readmission in women with history of psychotic and bipolar disorders.

Please note that the Becoming Model is not suitable for parents with a history of severe mental illness. Exploring history of mental health with any client should be done carefully and by employing one's clinical judgment, especially within the perinatal period. Also, important to note that childbirth is a process that can trigger the acute onset of psychoses as mentioned in the quote above by Taylor et al. (2019). Hence this sub-theme is a reminder to the therapist that anything is possible within the perinatal period when it comes to mental health. Such as even a person without an eventful mental health history can suffer from an acute onset of psychoses after birth.

Therapists working with perinatal clients also need to consider client's history of non-psychotic disorders. The following is a quote from another latest systematic literature review outlining the risk of relapse and onset of non-psychotic affective disorders in the perinatal period (Conejo-Galindo et al., 2022).

> Pregnancy is a critical period, both physiologically and emotionally, with an increased likelihood of relapse. Although much uncertainty still remains about the risk of mood episodes during pregnancy…women with a history of BD are at high risk for postpartum relapse…Postpartum is a period of high risk for the appearance and recurrence of psychiatric disorders, particularly depression, mania, and psychoses…Episodes of hypomania, mania, or depression may occur in the context of BD or develop for the first time after childbirth…Childbirth can also be the trigger for bipolar depression.

Living with chronic condition and caring

As illustrated so far, the perinatal period is certainly full of surprises. Especially when it comes to one's mental health, one's existing physical illness or chronic conditions can impact the person significantly. There is an ample amount of research available in the area of the impact of caring while living with chronic conditions which includes issues such as carer's fatigue, caregiver's stress, burnout, etc. They are useful in understanding the importance of exploring medical history and physical conditions when it comes to its impact on the person in general (Rothrauff et al., 2009). Knowledge from this area of research is highly transferable and useful for perinatal counselling. Because such research data helps us understand the impact that chronic disease may have on one's caring role and on their life in general. Considering how stressful it might be for a caregiver to mind someone while living with chronic condition, it is highly relevant to explore the experience of a person living with chronic condition and going through the perinatal period. However, please note that while the terms "parent" and "caregiver" are often used interchangeably, both are not the same. A parent is mostly the main caregiver(s) of the child. However, not all parents are the primary caregivers. At the same time, not all caregivers are parents, some are contracted and employed to care for the child.

Living with a chronic condition and looking after young children and/or household duties and/or others such as partner and other family members (e.g., sibling(s), elderly parent(s)) is highly stressful. In most cases, the person will experience physical and emotional stress which may include some of the following symptoms (Woods, 2014).

> Anger, sometimes leading to physical violence, Anxiety, Denial, Depression, Dissatisfaction with life, Exhaustion, Guilt, Irritability Stress-related physical conditions, such as gastrointestinal problems or insomnia.

Caregivers who have multiple roles will have different stressors based on the intensity of the multiple responsibilities, involvement and relationship they have with the person(s). According to Woods (2014) some of these stressors are:

> …extra demands on time and energy, changes in family roles and responsibilities, changes in work time and time to perform professional responsibilities, and pressure of trying to keep up with the caregiving and still having a life outside of work and the home.

The abovementioned stressors are also applicable to parents. This is true especially if they are returning to their employment, looking after other children and their household, have roles and duties as a partner, have other family members to provide care for and have a newborn or a new child in their family. Trying to wear different hats in different settings to different people is exhausting during the perinatal period. For instance, imagine being a kind parent to other children, a loving partner, an efficient employee, a supportive family member to others, a friendly neighbour, a fun friend and a new parent all at once! In addition, perhaps caring for elderly parents or unwell adult siblings and suffering from chronic diseases like high blood pressure or diabetes or chronic pain!

Multiple roles and exhaustion and chronic condition

Most perinatal clients will speak about their experience of exhaustion in some form or the other. However, when exploring this theme, the therapist is encouraged to address the level of exhaustion that the person may be experiencing from the broader context of serving multiple roles while living with chronic conditions and considering their previous medical and psychological history. This is an intersectional view of the person. This sub-theme aims to help the therapist have such a holistic view. Exhaustion is a highly relevant topic within this theme with a massive amount of literature available to draw from. However, exhaustion is also a theme that is omnipresent in all of the ten major themes of this model. Hence, this chapter will only mention the importance of addressing exhaustion as part of this theme but will not highlight any further literature on the topic. This topic is however explored again in Chapter 13 as part of the major theme Support System.

Conclusion

This chapter explored the major theme "History of previous diagnosis" and its two related sub-themes: Medical and Psychological. The chapter explored the sub-themes by drawing from some of the latest research literature on this topic and drew attention to the intersection of chronic conditions, caring, exhaustion and their impact on perinatal mental health. The next chapter will explore the major theme "Ongoing Risk".

References

CDC. (2023). About Chronic Diseases. Retrieved from https://www.cdc.gov/chronicdisease/about/index.htm

Conejo-Galindo, J., Sanz-Giancola, A., Álvarez-Mon, M., Ortega, M., Gutiérrez-Rojas, L., & Lahera, G. (2022). Postpartum relapse in patients with bipolar disorder. *Journal of Clinical Medicine, 11*(14), 3979. https://doi.org/10.3390/jcm11143979

Drinkaware. (2023). *Alcohol consumption in Ireland | drinkaware*. Retrieved March 30, 2023, from https://www.drinkaware.ie/research/alcohol-consumption-in-ireland/

Kaasbøll, J., Skokauskas, N., Lydersen, S., & Sund, A. M. (2021). Parental chronic illness, internalizing problems in young adulthood and the mediating role of adolescent attachment to parents: A prospective cohort study. *Frontiers in Psychiatry, 12*. https://doi.org/10.3389/fpsyt.2021.807563

Nichol, J. R., Sundjaja, J. H., & Nelson, G. (2022). Medical History. In *StatPearls*. StatPearls Publishing.

NCI. (2023). *Chronic Disease. NCI Dictionary of Cancer terms*. Retrieved March 30, 2023, from https://www.cancer.gov/publications/dictionaries/cancer-terms/def/chronic-disease

Rothrauff, T. C., Cooney, T. M., & An, J. S. (2009). Remembered parenting styles and adjustment in middle and late adulthood. *The Journals of Gerontology Series B: Psychological Sciences and Social Sciences, 64B*(1), 137–146. https://doi.org/10.1093/geronb/gbn008

Taylor, C. L., Stewart, R. J., & Howard, L. M. (2019). Relapse in the first three months post-partum in women with history of serious mental illness. *Schizophrenia Research, 204*, 46–54. https://doi.org/10.1016/j.schres.2018.07.037

Wharff, E., & Ginnis, K. (2007). Chapter 166 – assessment and management of suicidal patients. In L. Zaoutis & V. Chiang (Eds.), *Comprehensive pediatric Hospital medicine* (pp. 1046–1050). Mosby. https://doi.org/10.1016/B978-032303004-5.50170-8

WHO. (2023a). *Tobacco.* World Health Organization. Retrieved March 30, 2023, from https://www.who.int/news-room/fact-sheets/detail/tobacco

WHO. (2023b). *Physical activity.* World Health Organization. Retrieved March 30, 2023, from https://www.who.int/news-room/fact-sheets/detail/physical-activity

WHO. (2023c). *Fact sheets – malnutrition.* World Health Organisation. Retrieved March 30, 2023, from https://www.who.int/news-room/fact-sheets/detail/malnutrition

Woods, M. (2014). *Caregiver stress: The impact of chronic disease on the family.* Western New York Urology Associates. Retrieved March 30, 2023, from https://www.wnyurology.com/content.aspx?chunkiid=74397

Chapter 12

Ongoing Risks

Sub-themes:

a Aggression/abuse/coercive control/domestic violence
b Risks particular to socio-economic group
c Nationality/immigration status
d Religious/cultural

Introduction

This chapter will explore the major theme "Ongoing risk" and its related four sub-themes. The chapter will firstly outline three groupings of major risk factors at a glance such as biological, psychological and sociological risk factors. The chapter will then explore each sub-theme by providing definitions, prevalence and engaging with the most relevant official and/or latest literature on the topic. The main aim is to help the therapist understand the significance of risk assessment within this area. This will be done by providing a rationale for exploring the theme and its sub-themes, highlighting the complex intersections that may be otherwise missed and presenting a bird's eye view of the sub-themes by drawing from official sources and latest research relevant to the topics for the therapists to consider.

Risk factors at a glance

This theme aims to highlight some of the major psycho-social risk factors of perinatal well-being and the importance of assessing and addressing them in the therapeutic setting. The American Psychiatric Association (APA) Dictionary (APA 2023) defines "risk" in the following way.

> 1. the probability or likelihood that a negative event will occur, such as the risk that a disease or disorder will develop. 2. the probability of experiencing loss or harm that is associated with an action or behavior.

Perinatal well-being can be impacted by several physical, psychological and sociological risk factors. The sub-themes in this chapter will mainly focus on the sociological risk factors. However, some of the major bio-psycho-social risk factors are outlined below at a glance from a recent meta-analysis conducted by Blount et al. (2021). Some of them have been explored elsewhere in this book as major themes and sub-themes in other chapters.

1 Biological risk factors and their components

- Body changes, hormonal changes, medication concerns, epigenetic changes
- Poor nutrition, vitamin deficiencies, lack of access to quality food

DOI: 10.4324/9781003309710-13

- Neurological changes (e.g., brain structure changes), genetic predisposition to illness/health
- Negative/traumatic experiences of childhood

2 Psychological risk factors and their components: Past traumatic experiences influencing offspring

- Peri-partum: Anxiety, fatigue/exhaustion, baby blues, mood changes (in the last month of gestation or first few months after delivery)
- Post-partum: Baby blues, post-partum depression (PPD), depression, self-esteem issues, anxiety, stress, lack of support (in post-gestation)
- Stressors: Caused by biological components (e.g., physical changes, nutritional demands, neurobiological changes, traumatic events), mental wellness concerns, anxiety, lack of support, weathering phenomenon
- Transgenerational trauma: Past traumatic experiences influencing offspring

3 Sociological risk factors and their components

- Income/poverty: Lower SES associated with negative maternal and neonatal outcomes
- Discrimination: Unjust treatment, negative impacts on maternal and neonatal outcomes
- Race: Racial disparities in birth outcomes, most common form is verbal-based discrimination, Women of Colour (WOC) experience worse maternal and neonatal pregnancy lifecycle outcomes
- Relational aspects: Love, friendship, social support, intimate partner violence (IPV)
- Access to insurance/quality healthcare: Insurance plans, family planning access/reproductive care

a. Aggression/abuse/coercive control/domestic violence

This sub-theme includes some of the major risk factors from within the relational aspect in the perinatal period. There are several ways to assess these risk factors in therapeutic setting, and this section is not aimed at replicating or adding to those methods. Rather the following will aim to illustrate the importance of exploring them with perinatal clients. This is done by highlighting some of the key literature in this area to define these terms, illustrate their importance and outline their prevalence.

The APA Dictionary described "Aggression" in the following way and outlined three major types of aggression: hostile, instrumental and affective (APA, 2023).

…behavior aimed at harming others physically or psychologically. It can be distinguished from anger in that anger is oriented at overcoming the target but not necessarily through harm or destruction. When such behavior is purposively performed with the primary goal of intentional injury or destruction, it is termed **hostile aggression**. Other types of aggression are less deliberately damaging and may be instrumentally motivated (proactive) or affectively motivated (reactive). **Instrumental aggression** involves an action carried out principally to achieve another goal, such as acquiring a desired resource. **Affective aggression** involves an emotional response that tends to be targeted toward the perceived source of the distress but may be displaced onto other people or objects if the disturbing agent cannot be attacked (see displaced aggression)…

The APA Dictionary further outlined Kenneth Moyer's (1968) classification of aggression and noted the following (APA, 2023).

> It describes predatory aggression to obtain food and the converse antipredatory aggression, territorial aggression to repel intruders from an area, intermale aggression against a competitor, fear-induced aggression, **irritable aggression** in response to pain or deprivation of an item required for survival, sexual aggression to secure mates, maternal aggression to protect young offspring, and instrumental aggression. See also dominance aggression.

The abovementioned types of aggression provide a snapshot of the variety of theoretical frameworks widely accepted and researched within the field of mental health. Transmission of this knowledge to the perinatal mental health field is beneficial to both the person and the clinician in exploring the nuances of the perinatal period. Aggression within the perinatal period is bi-directional: Both partners being aggressive to one another during pregnancy and postpartum. However, most research have access only to data on unidirectional aggression: Male to female during pregnancy and postpartum. Hence, while reading research on this topic, it is beneficial to note if the data collected is unidirectional or bidirectional and whether the researchers have outlined the distinction in their study or in their section on limitation of the study.

Note that in the clinic, the client usually refers to their behaviour as "anger" rather than "aggression". It is up to the clinician to assess and address aggression. Clinical experience from this field has taught us that in most cases aggression from the female parent towards children or their partner during the perinatal period can be conceptualised as a displaced reaction and as a distorted version of various complex emotions such as frustration, resentment, feeling lonely, feeling unacknowledged and more. These reactions can arise due to a variety of perceived or actual experiences such as unfair treatment, sense of inequality relevant to gendered roles and/or expectations related to one's gender and variety of recent changes such as changes in one's routine, changes in one's body, their environment, their access to leisure time, their freedom, etc., to name few. Most parents (both male and female) attending therapy during the perinatal period have disclosed that they have felt aggression towards their children on several occasions. However, in most cases, the female parents had more complex and varied thought processes behind their aggression. Below are some examples.

In some cases, it was revealed that the aggression had links to how the person was making sense of the contrast between their own experience of being parented and their child's experience of being parented. For instance, in one case, the mother recalled how she was not given attention and shown kindness as a child. She highlighted the contrast between her experience of being parented and how she paints her child, how she gives the attention and kindness. She highlighted how she was not given the opportunities to excel, grow and succeed. In contrast to how she gives those opportunities to her child. These contrasting experiences made her feel frustrated and angry. The frustration, in this case, arose from the felt sense of unfairness towards her as a child, compared to what her child is receiving. This had a ripple effect. She would feel "rage" as she would call it when the child would misbehave and not listen to her. Her frustration was expressed as displaced and inappropriate aggressive responses towards her 3 year child who would make general mistakes such as spilling, not eating when offered, not listening when asked to do something, etc. The mother explained that the anger she felt was associated to these unspoken thoughts in her mind: "I wasn't given half of what you get, why would you still ignore me?", "You don't know how fortunate you are", "If I didn't get compassion after being so compliant to my parents, you don't deserve compassion from yours", "why didn't I get compassion from my parents, where did I go wrong, why was I deprived of love?". These thoughts would flood in her head within seconds and she would scream at the child for simple mistakes.

In other cases, where mothers have disclosed situations of displaced anger, the thoughts in their head revealed in therapy were mostly as follows: "How is it fair that I have nothing else anymore except a baby that I am supposed to breastfeed but he gets to go to his job, chat to adults, gets to go golfing, gets to sleep and take naps, gets to buy stuff from amazon with his surplus sitting in his account, all the while I can't sleep, can't take naps and have to do all the household chores, plus mind the baby who just won't stop crying!".

In some other cases, mothers have revealed thoughts behind their aggression as the following: "I must be stupid, intolerant and a bad mother to complain at all because sure don't every other mother do this and never complain?". This type of thought has led to further feelings of guilt for many, and in those cases, the emotions were expressed in several unhealthy ways such as aggression and other inappropriate behaviour towards children, partner and self. It is thus important to explore whether anger or aggression is at all a relevant topic in the household in the person's history and current life.

Recognising the signs of abuse within the perinatal period, especially bidirectional (both partners being abusive to one another) and/or multidirectional abuse (towards child/children and others including partner and self) is imperative for the well-being and safety of all involved. The APA dictionary defines abuse as below (APA, 2023).

interactions in which one person behaves in a cruel, violent, demeaning, or invasive manner toward another person or an animal. The term most commonly implies physical mistreatment but also encompasses sexual and psychological (emotional) mistreatment.

The World Health Organization (WHO, 2012) outlined the issue of gender in relation to the topic of abuse within IPV in the following way.

> Although women can be violent in relationships with men, often in self-defence, and violence sometimes occurs in same-sex partnerships, the most common perpetrators of violence against women are male intimate partners or ex-partners (1). By contrast, men are far more likely to experience violent acts by strangers or acquaintances than by someone close to them (2).

Approximately one in three women will experience IPV in their lifetime (Devries et al., 2013). The WHO (2012) defined IPV as "any behaviour within an intimate relationship that causes physical, psychological or sexual harm to those in the relationship". The WHO further outlined four types of abuse relevant to IPV:

Physical violence, such as slapping, hitting, kicking and beating
Sexual violence, including forced sexual intercourse and other forms of sexual coercion
Emotional (psychological) abuse, such as insults, belittling, constant humiliation, intimidation (e.g., destroying things), threats of harm and threats to take away children
Controlling behaviours, including isolating a person from family and friends; monitoring their movements and restricting access to financial resources, employment, education or medical care

Please note that abuse in the household is often referred as "domestic violence" (WHO, 2012). However, the WHO clarified that abuse can be of several other types (WHO, 2012).

> 'domestic violence' is used in many countries to refer to partner violence but the term can also encompass child or elder abuse, or abuse by any member of a household.

Perez et al. (2022) in their latest systematic review outlined IPV and its prevalence in the following way.

> Intimate partner violence (IPV) has serious consequences, particularly during high-risk periods such as pregnancy, which poses a significant risk to maternal mental health. However, it is unclear whether IPV presents a broad risk for psychopathology or is specific to distinct diagnoses or symptom dimensions (e.g., panic, social anxiety)...the relative impact of physical versus psychological aggression remains unclear...Rates of psychological aggression, which may be especially detrimental to mental health, are particularly high, with an estimated

> 75–80% of couples engaging in psychologically aggressive acts during arguments…IPV rates during pregnancy…are nearly identical to lifetime rates… both mothers and fathers in psychologically aggressive relationships were prone to experiencing greater ill temper (anger/hostility)…

A recent Systematic review conducted by Mojahed et al. (2021) outlined further prevalence of IPV in the following way.

> Intimate partner violence (IPV) affects individuals and families from all backgrounds, regardless of their ethnicity, socio-economic status, sexual orientation, or religion. Pregnancy and childbirth could be a time of vulnerability to violence because of changes in physical, emotional, social, and economic demands and needs…[found] lower overall prevalence rates for unidirectional IPV postpartum (range: 2–58%) compared to pregnancy (range: 1.5–66.9%). Psychological violence was found to be the most prevalent form of violence during the entire perinatal period.

Finally, coercive control is another risk factor that needs to be paid attention to within the perinatal period. Since there are very little training and emphasis on it in general, clinicians often miss the tell-tale or warning signs. The APA Dictionary described coercion as below (APA, 2023).

> …the process of attempting to influence another person through the use of threats, punishment, force, direct pressure, and other negative forms of power.

Coercive behaviour outlined in the APA Dictionary comes with the following example (APA, 2023).

> …behavior designed to force others to do one's bidding, often masked as filial devotion or as marital or parental concern and sometimes expressed directly.
> (e.g., "If you don't do what I say, I'll kill myself").

Coercive control is now a criminal offence in several countries including Ireland since 1 January 2019. While a person could have been subjected to coercive control before 2019, their perpetrators cannot be prosecuted unless coercive control was exercised after 1 January 2019. Below is a snippet of how coercive control is defined by the An Garda Síochána (2019), Ireland's National Police and Security Service.

> Coercive Control is a persistent pattern of controlling, coercive and threatening behaviour including all or some forms of domestic abuse (emotional, physical, financial, sexual including threats) by a boyfriend/girlfriend, partner, husband/ wife or ex-partner.
> This can have a serious impact including the fear of violence, cause serious alarm and distress and can result in a person giving up work, changing their

routines, losing contact with family and friends. Coercive control can damage a person's physical and emotional well-being.

Coercive control can be difficult to detect from the outside looking into a relationship, so too can it be hard to spot when in the relationship itself. As the behaviour worsens and each iteration of abuse becomes a new normal, low self-esteem is just one of the many factors that can stop victims from seeing the reality of their situation.

The relevant persons when considering coercive control are: "a spouse or civil partner" and/or "not a spouse, civil partner, or related to the other person but is or was in an intimate relationship with that other person" (An Garda Síochána, 2019).

Therapists working with perinatal clients should be well-versed in understanding and assessing coercive control within the perinatal period. While it is up to the therapists and their training as to how they phrase their questions or enquire into this topic, below are the signs that the An Garda Síochána asked people to look out for in order to self-assess whether they are being a victim of coercive control (An Garda Síochána, 2019).

Does your partner/ex-partner:

- Isolate you from friends and family
- Deprive you of basic needs, such as food, electricity, and heating
- Monitor your time and behaviours
- Monitor you via online communication tools or spyware
- Take control over aspects of your everyday life, such as where you can go, who you can see, what you can wear, when to be home and when you can sleep
- Deprive you access to support services, including medical services
- Repeatedly put you down, for example, saying "you're worthless"
- Humiliate, degrade or dehumanise you
- Control your finances
- Make threats or intimidate you
- Damage belongings
- Subject you to sexual abuse and/or physical violence

The following are the signs that An Garda Síochána (2019) asks people to look out for to assess if someone they know is being a victim of coercive control.

Do they:

- Appear frightened of their partner/ex-partner
- Appear isolated from family and friends
- Show signs of a change in behaviour, for example, more withdrawn, have low self-esteem and/or appear anxious or depressed
- Make excuses for their partner's abusive behaviour
- Have unexplained bruises or cuts

- Continually get phone calls or texts from their partner/ex-partner, wanting to know where they are and whom they're with
- Appears defensive or concerned about engaging with Gardaí

b. Risks particular to socio-economic group

As part of the biopsychosocial model, it is crucial that the person's social aspects are addressed and the ways they may impact the person's life within the perinatal period are explored. This should be done in line with the therapist's own training and within the context of their client's situation. The following is aimed at providing some key aspects of this topic for the therapist's consideration. There are several research studies examining the connections between postnatal depression and sociodemographic risk factors. For instance, a large population-based cross-sectional study conducted in Sydney, Australia outlined the following risk factors (Eastwood et al., 2011).

> ...difficult financial situation, living in the suburb one year or less, 'no regret leaving the suburb', unplanned pregnancy, not breastfeeding, and poor rating of mother's own health. Other social demographic factors such as marital status, maternal age, education of mother, or being Aboriginal or a Torres Strait Islander show no significant association with postnatal depressive symptoms... Neighbourhood and community group-level factors may be important and should be studied further.

There are several studies researching relationship status as a mediator of mental health outcome within the perinatal period. One such study was conducted in Edinburgh, UK, and they found the following when they compared Edinburgh Postnatal Depression Scales (EPDS) Scores among their women participants (Bilszta et al., 2008).

> Women in a partnered-relationship with poor partner-derived support were at an increased risk of elevated antenatal EPDS scores compared to single/unpartnered women. A previous history of depression and current emotional problems, rather than single mother status, were significant risk factors for elevated EPDS scores.

There are several ways to examine the connections between perinatal mental health and socio-economic status to identify risk factors such as gender, relationship status, income, age, education and so on. It is the therapist who would decide based on their training and clinical judgment as to how they would approach this subject. The following is how, at a very basic level, socio-economic groups are understood at a government level in Ireland. The Central Statistics Office in Ireland (CSO, 2016) outlined ten groupings in the following way.

> Socio-economic Group classifies the entire population into one of ten categories based on the level of skill and educational attainment of their occupation (those

at work, unemployed or retired). All other people are classified to the socio-economic group of the person in the family on whom they are deemed to be dependent.

The Central Statistics Office outlined the following ten socio-economic groups based on occupation and a separate group for the rest of the population (CSO, 2016).

1   Employers and managers
2   Higer professionals
3   Lower professionals
4   Non-manual
5   Manual-skilled
6   Semi-skilled
7   Unskilled
8   Own account workers
9   Farmers
10 Agricultural workers
11 All others gainfully occupied and unknown

The Central Statistics Office in Ireland further classified seven groups in the following way (CSO, 2016).

The entire population is also classified into one of seven social class groups which are ranked on the basis of occupation, thereby bringing together people with similar levels of occupational skill.

These seven groups are as follows:

1 Professional workers
2 Managerial technical
3 Non-manual
4 Skilled manual
5 Semi-skilled
6 Unskilled
7 All other gainfully occupied and unknown

While the above may serve as guidelines to understand some aspects of a person's socio-demography, the field of Sociology however has taught us how difficult it is to work with the concept of "class". Everyone knows what it is and yet our language escapes to define this concept. The discipline of Sociology has dedicated itself from the dawn of its existence in understanding what "class" or "social class" is and yet there are no consensus on this topic. Hence, therapists working within this area trying to understand how one's demography or socio-economic status or class may have an impact on their well-being and mental health, especially during the perinatal period must consider the complexities of defining these terms.

There are however inequalities in both the fields of physical health and mental health. The Black Report (Gray, 1982) named after the chairman of the study Sir Douglas Black, who was the President of the Royal College of Physicians at that time, outlined four main factors explaining the inequalities in health. Rogers and Pilgrim (2005) summarised these four categories in the following way:

1 Artefact explanations: Inequalities are explained via the artefact lens. Rogers and Pilgrim (2005, p. 45) clarified that "By implication the artefact explanation attacks the assumption that health inequalities exist at all and that there is a causal relationship between social conditions and health".
2 Selection explanations: The hypothesis is that "long-term illness or 'health capital' in early life constrains social mobility and continued inequalities in illness in adulthood...health status determines socio-economic position..." (Rogers & Pilgrim, 2005, p. 45). This is similar to the sociological concept of "Social Drift" theory where those who argue *for* this theory claim, "that mentally ill people drift into poverty" and those who argue *against* the theory claim, "that poverty precipitates illness" (Rogers & Pilgrim, 2005, p. 47).
3 Cultural/behavioural explanations: This refers to a hypothesis that "suggest that lifestyle and health-related behaviours (such as cigarette smoking, diet and lack of exercise among manual groups) lead to health inequalities" (Rogers & Pilgrim, 2005, p. 45).
4 Materialist explanations: This hypothesis highlights "the differential exposure to health threats inherent in society over which people have little control" (Rogers & Pilgrim, 2005, p. 45). This theory suggests "that a person's socio-economic position, and material deprivation in particular, leads to poorer health among people in lower social classes" (Rogers & Pilgrim, 2005, p. 45).

The therapist's worldview, their own experience and training background will determine what or if any of these hypotheses they align with in terms of the explanation for health inequalities. However, the purpose of highlighting this cross-disciplinary knowledge in this chapter is solely to encourage the therapist to remain open and inquisitive about the connections between one's socio-economic status and their mental health during the perinatal period, particularly with a view to assess and address the possible risk factors.

When engaging in research within this intersection of perinatal mental health and socio-economic status, one must consider the following aspect outlined by Rogers and Pilgrim (2005, p. 50) in their seminal text titled *"Sociology of Mental Health and illness"*.

In most epidemiological studies there has been a tendency to treat the socioeconomic status of individuals as a proxy for the social contexts in which they live (and vice versa). For example, we assume that poor people only live in poor areas and in poor areas there are only poor people. However, this can lead to the 'ecological fallacy' – the mistake of assuming that there are no individual class differences within specified localities. This fallacy may be particularly evident in large cities, such as London, containing many socially 'mixed' areas. At the same time, there is some evidence that many cities and towns indeed have environmentally differentiated areas, even though the social boundary between them may be the difference between one street and the next (Macintyre, Ellaway and Cummins 2002). The distinct environmental features impact on all residents (independent of their class position or socio-economic status). In poor areas these features include a high combination of environmental stressors and the relative absence of opportunities for healthy behaviour. For example, if people are fearful of leaving their homes, then they will not go out walking or make social contacts regularly. Thus neighbourhood seems to have an independent effect on mental health. This suggests the need to distinguish between individually defined and neighbourhood-defined social position, as sources of mental distress.

c. Nationality/immigration status

This sub-theme aims to explore the implication of immigration status on the person's mental health during the perinatal period. In the Guidance on Perinatal Mental Health, an official document published by the Government of the United Kingdom (Public Health England, 2019), the following risk factors for particularly postnatal depression were outlined.

- History of mental health problems
- Childhood abuse and neglect
- Domestic violence
- Interpersonal conflict
- Inadequate social support
- Alcohol or drug abuse
- Unplanned or unwanted pregnancy
- Migration status

As indicated above, the person's migration status is one of the significant risk factors, and it is considered one of the mediators in the person's mental health outcome within the perinatal period. The following is aimed at capturing some of the key definitions relevant to this theme for the ease of the therapist to explore further using their own techniques and clinical judgment.

The European Commission (2023) defines Migration as below.

In the *global context*, movement of a person either across an international border (international migration), or within a state (internal migration) for more than one year irrespective of the causes, voluntary or involuntary, and the means, regular or irregular, used to migrate.

The International Organization for Migration (IOM, 2019) outlined the following categories and definitions as there can be several different types of migration:

- **Circular migration:** A form of migration in which people repeatedly move back and forth between two or more countries (IOM, 2019, p. 29)
- **Climate migration:** The movement of a person or groups of persons who, predominantly for reasons of sudden or progressive change in the environment due to climate change, are obliged to leave their habitual place of residence, or choose to do so, either temporarily or permanently, within a State or across an international border (IOM, 2019, p. 31).
- **Displacement**: The movement of persons who have been forced or obliged to flee or to leave their homes or places of habitual residence, in particular as a result of or in order to avoid the effects of armed conflict, situations of generalized violence, violations of human rights or natural or human-made disasters (IOM, 2019, p. 55).
- **Economic migration**: The movement of a person or a group of persons, either across an international border or within a State motivated solely or primarily by economic opportunities (IOM, 2019, p. 62).
- **Facilitated migration:** Regular migration that has been encouraged or supported by State policies and practices or by the direct assistance of international organizations to make the act of migration and residence easier, more transparent and more convenient (IOM, 2019, p. 71).
- **Family migration**: A general concept covering: (1) family reunification of spouse, parent, children or other relatives; (2) family formation or new marriage of a migrant with permanent residents or citizens or (3) family accompanying a family member entering at the same time as primary migrant (IOM, 2019, p. 71).
- **Forced migration**: A migratory movement which, although the drivers can be diverse, involves force, compulsion or coercion (IOM, 2019, p. 77).
- **Internal migration:** The movement of people within a State involving the establishment of a new temporary or permanent residence (IOM, 2019, p. 108).
- **International migration**: The movement of persons away from their place of usual residence and across an international border to a country of which they are not nationals (IOM, 2019, p. 113).
- **Irregular migration:** Movement of persons that takes place outside the laws, regulations or international agreements governing the entry into or exit from the State of origin, transit or destination (IOM, 2019, p. 116).
- **Labour migration**: Movement of persons from one State to another, or within their own country of residence, for the purpose of employment (p. 123).
- **Mixed migration:** A movement in which a number of people are travelling together, generally in an irregular manner, using the same routes and means of transport, but for different reasons. People travelling as part of mixed movements have varying needs and profiles and may include asylum seekers, refugees, trafficked persons, unaccompanied/separated children and migrants in an irregular situation (IOM, 2019, p. 141).

- **Safe, orderly and regular migration:** Movement of persons in keeping both with the laws and regulations governing exit from, entry and return to and stay in States and with States' international law obligations, in a manner in which the human dignity and well-being of migrants are upheld, their rights are respected, protected and fulfilled and the risks associated with the movement of people are acknowledged and mitigated (IOM, 2019, p. 191).
- **Return migration:** In the context of international migration, the movement of persons returning to their country of origin after having moved away from their place of habitual residence and crossed an international border. In the context of internal migration, the movement of persons returning to their place of habitual residence after having moved away from it (IOM, 2019, p. 186).

Some other common terminologies that are relevant to this theme are the following:

- **Asylum seeker**: An individual who is seeking international protection. In countries with individualized procedures, an asylum seeker is someone whose claim has not yet been finally decided on by the country in which he or she has submitted it. Not every asylum seeker will ultimately be recognized as a refugee, but every recognized refugee is initially an asylum seeker (IOM, 2019, p. 14).
- **Asylum Diplomatic**: Refuge that States grant beyond the boundaries of their territory, in places in which they benefit from immunity from jurisdiction of the territorial State, to an individual seeking protection (IOM, 2019, p. 13).
- **Refugee (mandate):** A person who qualifies for the protection of the United Nations provided by the High Commissioner for Refugees (UNHCR), in accordance with UNHCR's Statute and, notably, subsequent General Assembly's resolutions clarifying the scope of UNHCR's competency, regardless of whether or not he or she is in a country that is a party to the 1951 Convention or the 1967 Protocol – or a relevant regional refugee instrument – or whether or not he or she has been recognized by his or her host country as a refugee under either of these instruments (IOM, 2019, p. 170).
- **International Protection:** The protection that is accorded by the international community to individuals or groups who are outside their own country and are unable to return home because their return would infringe upon the principle of non-refoulement, and their country is unable or unwilling to protect them (IOM, 2019, p. 114).
- **Immigrant:** From the perspective of the country of arrival, a person who moves into a country other than that of his or her nationality or usual residence, so that the country of destination effectively becomes his or her new country of usual residence (IOM, 2019, p. 103).
- **Emigrant:** From the perspective of the country of departure, a person who moves from his or her country of nationality or usual residence to another country, so that the country of destination effectively becomes his or her new country of usual residence (IOM, 2019, p. 63).

The above categories highlight the very fact that there are several different types of migration and that each one of them poses legal and/or social and/or psychosocial complexities. One can be in any of these situations or other situations that are not addressed here during their perinatal period. It is important that the therapist does not assume the implications of the situation going by terminologies that the client has used. It is always best practice to ask the client to explain the terminology, even if the therapist is well-versed in that topic. It is important that the therapist does not assume that their previous knowledge of those terminologies are sufficient as this is an ever-evolving dynamic field where new law and regulations come in often, replacing the previous legislations or guidance. Hence, it is essential that the therapist remains open to learning and be guided by their client in understanding the complexities and implications of the person's migration status.

In addition note that a person's migration status, experience of domestic violence, availability of social support and their mental health intersect. This intersection produces a complex environment for the person impacting their mental health further during their perinatal period. For example, clinical experience has taught us that many migrant women and sometimes men and those who do not identify as either continue to stay in abusive relationships during their perinatal period for a number of reasons including their migration status. This is true, especially in cases where they are waiting for their "green card" or equivalent or their turn to qualify for citizenship. The fear of their migration status being negatively impacted stop them from speaking out. This is an added stress on top of being socially isolated from friends and family as they do not have their own parents/family/friends around during their perinatal period in the country where they are currently residing. These are stressors that are highly significant to consider in addition to their journey of becoming a mother/father/parent.

d. Religious/cultural

This sub-theme explores the implication of the religious and cultural elements on the person's mental health during their perinatal period. Considering the complexity and depth of this subject area, this section will only draw from the area of religious coping. Engaging in spirituality and religion can be one of the tendencies that some people have during their perinatal period to cope with depression and anxiety. This is referred to as religious coping. Research on such religious coping yields mixed results because religious coping can be "multidimensional" according to Bakır et al. (2021). In their review, they highlighted the following, "Positive religious coping is associated with favourable benefits in the psychosocial adjustment, whereas negative religious coping leads to bad outcomes and therefore is deemed maladaptive…" (Bakır et al., 2021, p. 3379). Negative religious coping may work as a risk factor to the person's mental health and increase the symptoms of depression and anxiety rather than working as a protective factor during their perinatal period. The APA Dictionary defined "religion" in the following way.

> a system of spiritual beliefs, practices, or both, typically organized around the worship of an all-powerful deity (or deities) and involving behaviors such as prayer, meditation, and participation in collective rituals. Other common features of organized religions are the belief that certain moral teachings have divine authority, and the recognition of certain people, places, texts, or objects as holy or sacred.

Religion and mental health have a long complicated history. Michel Foucault has dedicated his life to examining this intersection, and some of his research has been captured in the *History of Madness* (Foucault, [1961] 2013), a seminal text for anyone working within the allied health profession, especially relevant for psychologists, psychiatrists, psychotherapists and counsellor. Clinical experience has taught us that one of the several aspects of religion that can impact someone negatively is a sense of extreme guilt and remorse.

Consider the concept of "Catholic guilt", a controversial phrase often colloquially used by native Irish clients. Within the Irish context, this phrase refers to a set of behaviour, emotions and thought processes that the person believe is associated to their cultural environment such as their catholic upbringing or the impact of the catholic church. Within the perinatal period, such an upbringing may add further complexities. This is similar to Islam and other religion where clients have often interpreted the concept of guilt as something that takes priority over their own wellbeing. From clinical experience, it seems that the following situations are the major instances where religion was identified as a risk factor within the perinatal period: Unwanted pregnancy (variety of reasons), sex outside marriage resulting in pregnancy, struggling to feel a sense of bonding with the infant, wishing to leave marriage during the perinatal period for several reasons including domestic violence and abuse, having a child with someone who does not share the same religious and cultural values, not being able to practice own religious or cultural values due to several reasons and many more. The sense of guilt experienced by the person arising from their own religious and cultural beliefs in these situations seemed significantly higher than other risk factors and these factors were negatively impacting their mental health during their perinatal period. However, there have also been clients who found their religious and cultural beliefs to be working as a protective factor during their perinatal period, but not during the instances outlined above.

In addition, there is another concept that is highly relevant to this sub-theme: Honour-based abuse (HBA). The Metropolitan Police in the United Kingdom outlined the following on HBA (MET, 2023).

Have you been threatened or abused if you've tried to:

- Have a relationship or marry someone outside your community or someone within your community that your family don't approve of

- Separate or divorce
- Talk to certain people
- Have sex before marriage
- Become pregnant or give birth outside of marriage
- Wear clothes your family or community think are inappropriate
- Use drugs or alcohol
- Access higher education
- Challenge what your family or community expect of you
- Disagree with the religion of your family or community

People who carry out HBA are often close family members but also extended family or community members.

HBA has increased by at least 81% in the last five years according to the Guardian newspaper (Siddique, 2021). Most of the above signs correlate highly with one's perinatal period. When considering the different types of HBA outlined by the Metropolitan Police, it becomes much more obvious that the interactions between religion, culture, social support, domestic violence, gender, immigration status, socio-economic status and perinatal mental health are crucial to consider as risk factors (MET, 2023).

There isn't one specific crime of HBA. It can involve a range of crimes and behaviours, such as:

- Forced marriage
- Domestic abuse (physical, sexual, psychological, emotional or financial)
- Sexual harassment and sexual violence (rape and sexual assault or the threat of)
- Threats to kill, physical and emotional violence and murder
- Pressure to go or move abroad
- Being kept at home with no freedom
- Not allowed to use the telephone, internet, or have access to important documents like your passport or birth certificate
- Isolation from friends and members of your own family

Conclusion

This chapter explored the major theme "Ongoing risk" and its related four sub-themes. The chapter outlined three major groupings of risk factors at a glance and focused on psychosocial risk factors. The chapter provided definitions and snippets of the latest research and literature from official sources relevant to the four sub-themes. Drawing from clinical experience, the chapter highlighted the rationale for the inclusion of this theme and some of the complex intersections within this field that may remain unexplored otherwise but have the potential to contribute to perinatal distress. The next chapter will focus on the last major theme of this model "Support system".

References

An Garda Síochána. (2019). *What is coercive control? An Garda Síochána.* Retrieved April 1, 2023, from https://www.garda.ie/en/crime/domestic-abuse/what-is-coercive-control-.html

APA. (2023). APA Dictionary of Psychology. Retrieved from https://dictionary.apa.org/

Bakır, N., Irmak Vural, P., & Demir, C. (2021). Relationship of depression, anxiety and stress levels with religious coping strategies among Turkish pregnant women during the COVID-19 pandemic. *Journal of Religion and Health, 60*(5), 3379–3393. https://doi.org/10.1007/s10943-021-01391-7

Bilszta, J. L., Tang, M., Meyer, D., Milgrom, J., Ericksen, J., & Buist, A. E. (2008). Single motherhood versus poor partner relationship: Outcomes for antenatal mental health. *Australian & New Zealand Journal of Psychiatry, 42*(1), 56–65. https://doi.org/10.1080/00048670701732731

Blount, A. J., Adams, C. R., Anderson-Berry, A. L., Hanson, C., Schneider, K., & Pendyala, G. (2021). Biopsychosocial factors during the perinatal period: Risks, preventative factors, and implications for healthcare professionals. *International Journal of Environmental Research and Public Health, 18*(15), 8206. https://doi.org/10.3390/ijerph18158206

CSO. (2016). *6. Socio-Economic Group and social class.* Central Statistics Office. Retrieved April 2, 2023, from https://www.cso.ie/en/media/csoie/newsevents/documents/census-2016summaryresultspart2/Chapter_6_Socio-economic_group_and_social_class.pdf

Devries, K. M., Mak, J. Y., Garcia-Moreno, C., Petzold, M., Child, J. C., Falder, G., & Watts, C. H. (2013). The global prevalence of intimate partner violence against women. *Science, 340*(6140), 1527–1528.

Eastwood, J. G., Phung, H., & Barnett, B. (2011). Postnatal depression and socio-demographic risk: Factors associated with Edinburgh depression scale scores in a metropolitan area of new South Wales, Australia. *Australian & New Zealand Journal of Psychiatry, 45*(12), 1040–1046. https://doi.org/10.3109/00048674.2011.619160

European Commission. (2023). *Migration.* Retrieved from https://home-affairs.ec.europa.eu/networks/european-migration-network-emn/emn-asylum-and-migration-glossary/glossary/migration_en

Foucault, M. (2013). *History of madness (1961).* Taylor and Francis.

Gray, A. M. (1982). Inequalities in health. The black report: A summary and comment. *International Journal of Health Services: Planning, Administration, Evaluation, 12*(3), 349–380. https://doi.org/10.2190/XXMM-JMQU-2A7Y-HX1E

IOM. (2019). *International Migration Law No. 34 – glossary on migration.* Retrieved April 2, 2023, from https://publications.iom.int/books/international-migration-law-ndeg34-glossary-migration

MET. (2023). *What is honour-based abuse? | metropolitan police.* Retrieved April 2, 2023, from https://www.met.police.uk/advice/advice-and-information/honour-based-abuse/honour-based-abuse/

Mojahed, A., Alaidarous, N., Kopp, M., Pogarell, A., Thiel, F., & Garthus-Niegel, S. (2021). Prevalence of intimate partner violence among intimate partners during the perinatal period: A narrative literature review. *Frontiers in Psychiatry, 12.* https://doi.org/10.3389/fpsyt.2021.601236

Moyer, K. (1968). Kinds of Aggression and Their Physiological Basis. *Communications In Behavioural Biology, 2*(2), 65–87. doi:https://www.ojp.gov/ncjrs/virtual-library/abstracts/kinds-aggression-and-their-physiological-basis

Perez, G. R., Stasik-O'Brien, S. M., Laifer, L. M., & Brock, R. L. (2022). Psychological and physical intimate partner aggression are associated with broad and specific internalizing symptoms during pregnancy. *International Journal of Environmental Research and Public Health*, *19*(3), 1662. https://doi.org/10.3390/ijerph19031662

Public Health England. (2019). *Mental health and wellbeing: 4. Perinatal Mental Health. JSNA toolkit*. Gov.uk. Retrieved April 2, 2023, from https://www.gov.uk/government/publications/better-mental-health-jsna-toolkit/4-perinatal-mental-health#fn:6

Rogers, A., & Pilgrim, D. (2005). *A sociology of mental health and illness*. McGraw-Hill Open University Press.

Siddique, H. (2021, October 31). Honour-based' offences soared by 81% in last five year. *The Guardian*. Retrieved from https://www.theguardian.com/society/2021/oct/31/honour-based-offences-soared-by-81-in-last-five-years

WHO. (2012). *Understanding and addressing violence against women: Intimate partner violence*. World Health Organization. Retrieved April 1, 2023, from https://www.who.int/publications-detail-redirect/WHO-RHR-12.36

Chapter 13

Support System

Sub-themes:

a   Access to family/friends
b   Economic independence
c   Location (rural, suburb, neighbours)
d   Help at home (e.g., sleep/rest)

Introduction

This chapter will explore the last major theme "Support system" and its related four sub-themes: Access to family/friends, Economic independence, Location (rural, suburb, neighbours) and Help at home (e.g., sleep/rest). The chapter will draw from official sources and relevant recent literature to highlight definitions and connections between the sub-themes and perinatal mental health.

Support

This theme is one of the most significant one among all the other themes of the Becoming Model. Having a good support system around can sometimes work as a protective shield against most of the common risk factors during the perinatal period. Social support is an all-encompassing term for a number of different elements and dimensions of support. The American Psychiatric Association (APA) Dictionary (APA, 2023) described social support in the following way.

> the provision of assistance or comfort to others, typically to help them cope with biological, psychological, and social stressors. Support may arise from any interpersonal relationship in an individual's social network, involving family members, friends, neighbors, religious institutions, colleagues, caregivers, or support groups. It may take the form of practical help (e.g., doing chores, offering advice), tangible support that involves giving money or other direct material assistance, and emotional support that allows the individual to feel valued, accepted, and understood.

Social support works as a protective factor in general population against depression and in the perinatal period it works "as a possible protective factor for coping with difficulties arising from the many challenges that motherhood brings" (Milgrom et al., 2019). In pregnancy, social support was found to be inversely associated with depressive symptoms, meaning decreased social support correlated with increased depressive symptoms and vice versa (Milgrom et al., 2019). Similarly, Bedaso et al.

DOI: 10.4324/9781003309710-14

(2021) noted the following from their findings, "low affectionate support/positive social interaction had a higher odds of anxiety symptoms compared to pregnant women who reported high affectionate support/positive social interaction". They further hypothesised the following (Bedaso et al., 2021).

> Pregnant women with low affectionate support/positive social interaction are less satisfied with family and poor in interacting with the social environment, and as a result, they might be exposed to loneliness, become less in emotional and stress coping ability and later become more anxious.

There are several theories and psychological explanations for anxiety, low mood and stress. Therapists working within this field will be guided by their own training and clinical judgement in making sense of the presenting issues in their clients. However, the purpose of this chapter is to highlight from the current research findings and literature that most scholars and researchers agree on the following. Less support and/or exposure to negative social interaction can count for a feeling of loneliness and stress, contributing to mental health difficulties during the perinatal period.

a. Access to family/friends

This sub-theme aims to explore the person's current access to support from family and friends and its impact on their mental health during their perinatal period. Social interaction and support from our social environment are crucial for our wellbeing during our entire lifespan. The COVID-19 pandemic was one of the most teachable moments in our human history. It highlighted in the most cruel ways as to how important the social element of our life is. We learnt how vulnerable and dependent we are as mortal human subjects on others around us for various types of support. This is because the world came to a halt and we were forced to be isolated. Alone in our little bubbles, we remained in the lockdown with or without limited support from the outside world. For most of us, this was the first time we felt the real terror of loneliness and the fear of not having support around us. A recent British study titled *Babies in Lockdown* (Saunders & Hogg, 2020 cited in Bridle et al., 2022) enquired parent's experiences of having children during the lockdown and found the following.

> A total of 87% of parents reported an increase in anxiety during the pandemic, and one of the compounding factors was the false information and advice given to pregnant women. The fear of infection, financial insecurity, social isolation, and the restrictions put on the partners and families of women/birthing people during antenatal and intrapartum care all added to reports of anxiety, confusion, and loss. The report found that 32% of families wanted help with their mental wellbeing. Those who had the highest levels of anxiety in relation to the

pandemic were Black/Black British (46%), Asian/Asian British (50%), parents
under 25 (54%), and parents with household incomes of less than £16k (55%).

The above snippet from their study highlights that several strands of thoughts led
to increased anxiety during the pandemic for the parents of new babies. However,
two things worth drawing from the quote above: (1) Lack of financial support/
stability, social isolation and not having families/partners around were contributing
to increased feelings of anxiety, confirming social support particularly from family/
friends are crucial components in perinatal mental health. (2) Those with minority
ethnicity, those who are young and those from lower socio-economic status were
the most vulnerable without support. In other words, intersectionality is a key in
understanding the role that support plays when it comes to perinatal mental health.
Marginalised and diverse populations are at the most risk during their perinatal
period as they may not have access to family and friends' support similar to others
for a variety of reasons. It is up to the therapist as to how they explore this topic, but
knowledge of intersectionality is crucial in exploring all of the themes highlighted
in this book, especially the sub-themes in this chapter.

b. Economic independence

This sub-theme aims to highlight the connection between money, such as one's
financial circumstances and their mental health within the perinatal period. Many
women choose to give up their career and job during their perinatal period. They
decide to stay home after they give birth and choose to be financially dependent on
their partner or significant others. Other decides to go back to work as soon as possible to avoid financial strain. Some women reveal in therapy that they are being
controlled as they are now financially dependent on the other. Others experience
anxiety not knowing how they will provide for their offspring with our without
support from the others. Some men too decide not to work too after the birth of
their child, as it financially makes more sense for them to stay back as the cost of
living and childcare are skyrocketing. Men too can and do experience that they are
financially being controlled. Everyone has a different situation and experience with
money despite how similar it may seem on the surface. Important is to highlight
that one's support system must include financial support for there to be any protective effect against depression, anxiety and stress during perinatal period. Hence,
financial independence is a significant topic to explore and understand the person's
experience and how it may be contributing to perinatal distress.

Poverty and financial strains negatively impact maternal mental health (Dijkstra-
Kersten et al., 2015; Marcil et al., 2020; Wickham et al., 2017). The mechanisms
that explain *how* the mind is impacted and *why* the depressive and anxiety symptoms increase are *not* studied enough. However, in a therapy room, we leave the hypotheses for the mechanisms as open-ended and lose. As therapists, we are guided
by our clients as to why and how it impacts them. Hence, the purpose of discussing

this sub-theme here is to *not* provide a reason as to *why*, but rather highlight that there *is* a strong connection between financial strain and perinatal mental health. Hence, it is an important aspect to explore with a perinatal client. Please note that financial strain is only one aspect of economic dependency. Other elements may include financial fear, financial worries, financial abuse and more. Although this is an under-researched area, the connection between money and mental health is well-researched and is available in accessible language for the general population (Mind, 2022).

c. Location (rural, suburb, neighbours)

This sub-theme highlights the connection between one's location and their mental health during their perinatal period. Current International research (high-, middle- and low-income countries) would suggest that women from rural areas are more likely to experience mental health difficulties in their perinatal period than their urban counterparts (Ginja et al., 2020). Some of the mediators for these differences may include the following factors (Ginja et al., 2020).

> difficulties in accessing healthcare services, regional variations in cultural practices, sociodemographic and lifestyle factors…varying levels of hazardous environmental, occupational and transportation conditions…Social support and socioeconomic status…

In the UK, in some areas neighbourhood deprivation theories have been linked to maternal mental health, especially in older mothers (Ginja et al., 2020). There are several external and internal factors that contribute to the rural-urban differences in mental health outcomes within the perinatal period. Clinical experience will show that in most cases it surmounts to a perceived sense of social isolation and actual access to amenities and/or friends and family. In that sense, rural community can make someone feel connected while urban individual living in apartments and estates can make someone feel isolated and lonely. Similarly, someone with access to family and friends closely, no matter where they live, can feel suffocated and wish to be living away from them, desiring freedom. It can also be the case that what once used to be home, may no longer seem as home. For instance, someone who has returned from years of working away to their neighbourhood to rear their family may realise that they do not feel the same about the place that they once called home. Hence, it is important to understand how the person's location is impacting their mental health and not to assume anything no matter how familiar the therapist may be with the latest research findings on this topic.

d. Help at home (e.g., sleep/rest)

This sub-theme refers to the most practical element of this model. The amount of support one has at home during their perinatal period will have an impact on their overall mood, physical health and mental health, especially during their pregnancy and at least the first five weeks postpartum. The one thing that any new parent miss the most and needs the most is, sleep and/or rest. For them to be able to sleep or rest, they need to have someone helping them, stepping in and supporting them. This sub-theme helps the therapist explore the client's current support structure at home and how much sleep/rest are they managing to get and what are the impacts on them of getting or not getting sleep/rest.

While this theme focuses on support that facilitates the parent to manage to get some sleep/rest, it is essential to note that the infant behavioural factor can add further complexities and negates the support that is offered or available. The infant's sleep patterns and problematic behaviour may mean that support is required more than usual or that other behaviour changes need to occur to restore sleep. This means support at home has to be multidimensional. Consider the following problems and the type of multidimensional support one needs to get to help them feel rested (Symon et al., 2012).

> Sleep problems in early infancy may have severe adverse consequences, including postnatal depression and maternal anxiety. Patterns that can be characterised as sleep problems include a range of behaviours such as frequent and long nocturnal awakenings, being nursed to sleep, taking prolonged periods to fall asleep, sharing a bed with the parent and only taking short naps during the day

The association between sleep quality and postpartum depression is well-researched. One's sleep pattern is hugely disturbed post a live birth. This is because infants usually have irregular sleep patterns, and there are biological and physiological implications on the mom post birth that impact their sleep. Moreover, if the person is breastfeeding, they will have further reasons for disrupted and irregular sleep. This will leave them exhausted and sleep deprived. In turn, sleep deprivation itself has physiological, biological and emotional consequences. Sleep and one's mood during the perinatal period are thus bidirectionally connected. There are several factors that impact the person's sleep both in their antenatal and postnatal period. However, support at home is one of the most common and prominent of them all. Having support at home means the person can catch up on their sleep at least a little and/or can feel rested while others help them with chores around the house including minding the baby. During the perinatal period, especially during the first few weeks post birth, any type of help at home can act as a protective shield against mental health difficulties and distress. This is because even an hour's nap or a shower or a healthy meal or even the vision of a clean kitchen counter and laundry washed, dried and folded in the cupboard can bring peace, making the person feel supported and cared for. This in turn can help them cope with further sleepless hours knowing that they have support and they aren't alone. Sleep deprivation is thus a huge factor that impacts a person negatively and having support at home can act as a mitigating factor against negative health and mental health outcome during the perinatal period. Iranpour et al. (2016) highlighted the association between sleep deprivation and mood disorders such as postnatal depression and confirmed the bidirectional connection between sleep and mood in the following way in their cross-sectional study.

> Sleep patterns and sleep deprivation are other potential factors which can be as-sociate with postpartum depression…Delivery has physical, physiological, and psychological effects on women's sleep, also taking care of a newborn with irregular sleep patterns will result in sleep disturbances during the postpar-tum period…especially in the first three postpartum months…insufficient and disrupted sleep affects memory, decision-making, psychomotor, and mood… association between depression and sleep can be bilateral. Depression may lead to disturbed sleep while sleep disorder can also be an independent risk factor for depression…

Support at home also depends on a number of factors that have been mentioned in previous chapters as other themes, such as couple's relationship or co-parenting factors, parenting style, worldviews, gender roles, ongoing risks and more. Please also note that it is not just about giving support or the availability of support, rather it is also about how one would receive or seek support. This is because not every-one knows how to and when to look for support. Support maybe easily available but someone may choose not to take it for a number of reasons that are unique to their situation. Moreover, a person's expectation of what "support" should look like and what they believe is a healthy way of looking for support will also depend on a number of factors but mainly on their own experience of being parented.

Conclusion

This chapter explored the major theme "Ongoing risk" and its related four sub-themes. The main aim of this chapter was to illustrate the connections between these sub-themes and perinatal mental health. The chapter did so by providing rationale for the inclusion of these sub-themes and providing definitions of the rel-evant terms by engaging with some of the recent literature on this topic. The next chapter will conclude this model.

References

American Psychological Association. (2023). APA Dictionary of Psychology. Retrieved from https://dictionary.apa.org/

Bedaso, A., Adams, J., Peng, W., & Sibbritt, D. (2021). The association between social sup-port and antenatal depressive and anxiety symptoms among Australian women. *BMC Pregnancy and Childbirth, 21*(1). https://doi.org/10.1186/s12884-021-04188-4

Bridle, L., Walton, L., van der Vord, T., Adebayo, O., Hall, S., Finlayson, E., Easter, A., & Silverio, S. A. (2022). Supporting perinatal mental health and wellbeing during COVID-19. *International Journal of Environmental Research and Public Health, 19*(3), 1777. https://doi.org/10.3390/ijerph19031777

Dijkstra-Kersten, S. M. A., Biesheuvel-Leliefeld, K. E. M., van der Wouden, J. C., Penninx, B. W. J. H., & van Marwijk, H. W. J. (2015). Associations of financial strain and income with depressive and anxiety disorders. *Journal of Epidemiology and Community Health, 69*(1), 660–665. https://doi.org/10.1136/jech-2014-205088

Ginja, S., Jackson, K., Newham, J. J., Henderson, E. J., Smart, D., & Lingam, R. (2020). Rural-urban differences in the mental health of perinatal women: A UK-based cross-sectional study. *BMC Pregnancy and Childbirth, 20*(1). https://doi.org/10.1186/s12884-020-03132-2

Iranpour, S., Kheirabadi, G. R., Esmaillzadeh, A., Heidari-Beni, M., & Maracy, M. R. (2016). Association between sleep quality and postpartum depression. *Journal of Research in Medical Sciences: The Official Journal of Isfahan University of Medical Sciences, 21*, 110, https://doi.org/10.4103/1735-1995.193500

Marcil, L. E., Campbell, J. I., Silva, K. E., Hughes, D., Salim, S., Nguyen, H. T., Kissler, K., Hole, M. K., Michelson, C. D., & Kistin, C. J. (2020). Women's experiences of the effect of financial strain on parenting and mental health. *Journal of Obstetric, Gynecologic, and Neonatal Nursing: JOGNN, 49*(6), 581–592. https://doi.org/10.1016/j.jogn.2020.07.002

Milgrom, J., Hirshler, Y., Reece, J., Holt, C., & Gemmill, A. W. (2019). Social support-a protective factor for depressed perinatal women. *International Journal of Environmental Research and Public Health, 16*(8), 1426. https://doi.org/10.3390/ijerph16081426

Mind. (2022). *Money and mental health.* mind.org.uk. Retrieved April 3, 2023, from https://www.mind.org.uk/media/12440/money-and-mental-health-2022-pdf.pdf

Saunders, B., & Hogg, S. (2020). *Babies in lockdown: Listening to parents to build back better.* Best Beginnings, Home-Start UK and The Parent-Infant Foundation.

Symon, B., Bammann, M., Crichton, G., Lowings, C., & Tucsok, J. (2012). Reducing postnatal depression, anxiety and stress using an infant sleep intervention [abstract]. *BMJ Open, 2*(5). https://doi.org/10.1136/bmjopen-2012-001662

Wickham, S., Whitehead, M., Taylor-Robinson, D., & Barr, B. (2017). The effect of a transition into poverty on child and maternal mental health: A longitudinal analysis of the UK millennium cohort study. *Lancet Public Health, 2*(3), e141–e148. https://doi.org/10.1016/S2468-2667(17)30011-7.

Chapter 14

Closing Remarks

This book has introduced the only integrative perinatal counselling model at the time of the drafting of this book. This book aimed to provide a much-needed clinical structure to therapists working within this field. Perinatal counselling is a distinct field that requires specialist knowledge and training. The Becoming model makes a significant contribution to that training. Drawing from both practice-based research and research-based practice, ten major themes and 40 sub-themes have been explored in each chapters. It is hoped that each theme provides the therapist with definitions, prevalence and a snippet of the most significant research findings on the topic. Each theme is to be only used as a road map and each chapter is written as a conversation starter for the therapists to use within the therapeutic settings with their perinatal clients.

The following is a snapshot of the chapters discussed in this book at a glance. Chapter 1 provided the definitions of the major terms used in this book and outlined the scope of the Becoming model. Chapter 2 provided the readers with rationale behind the name of the model and its distinct features. These information aimed at helping the therapist identify ways that are unique to them to integrate this model to their existing practice. Chapter 3 provided the readers with the visual representation of the Becoming model and outlined some of the some of the major theories that have been integrated to design this model. In addition, the chapter also laid out some of the basic assumptions underpinning this model. Chapter 4 explored the major theme of Identity. It outlined some of the major theories on maternal identity by drawing from some contemporary theorists' work from this small specialised clinical field. Some key concepts along with some possible questioning style were highlighted that may help the therapist explore the client's perception of themselves self as she transitions to motherhood. Chapter 5 explored the major theme of "Idea of motherhood/fatherhood – femininity/masculinity". The chapter illustrated how these terms can play a central role in the manifestation of most psychological difficulties and discomforts experienced in the perinatal period with or without the presence of a baby in one's life. The chapter provided a list of widely accepted definitions of these terms for the therapists to use as starting point to invite the client to explore this theme. Chapter 6 explored the theme of symbolic "Loss" and its six related sub-themes: Loss of

DOI: 10.4324/9781003309710-15

identity, Loss of freedom, Loss of personal space or privacy or alone time, Loss of spontaneity, Loss of social life or leisure time and Loss of desire and desirability. The chapter highlighted the central role that this theme can play in the manifestation of perinatal distress and mental health difficulties despite having delivered a healthy baby and leading a seemingly healthy and happy life. Major definitions of some of the terms used in this chapter and techniques of exploring these topics were outlined in the chapter for the therapist's considerations. Chapter 7 explored the major theme "Experience of conception, pregnancy and birth" and highlighted how these seemingly "natural" and "common-knowledge" elements are experienced by each person uniquely. The chapter is a reminder for the therapists to not assume any of these elements as standard. The chapter provided some basic facts about major complications and common terminologies relevant to these three major elements of the perinatal period. The aim was to encourage the therapist help the person explore their unique experience of these elements in therapy. Chapter 8 explored the major theme "Couple relationship and/or co-parenting relationship" and its related 13 sub-themes: From two to threesome, Parenting style differences, Differences in values, Differences in world-views, Perspectives on religion/ideals/ideologies, Perspectives on division of chores, Communication style, Role orientation, Coping styles and abilities, Sexual/intimacy (dis)satisfaction, Decision on finances, Conflicts about child rearing and Family history of distress (including trauma). This chapter outlined major definitions and snippets of current literature and theories relevant to these themes. The chapter highlighted how the unconscious perceptions, presuppositions, constructions and conscious experiences of and about these topics can contribute to perinatal distress and difficulties. Chapter 9 explored the theme "Experiences of being parented" and its four sub-themes: Dynamics between parents/caregivers, Trauma, estrangement, ACE, Current involvement or lack of and Parents/caregivers' parenting style. The chapter illustrated the importance of exploring these topics with perinatal clients as they transition to motherhood/fatherhood and provided snippets from recent literature on these topics such as definitions and major theories. Chapter 10 explored "Socio-economic background" and its related two sub-themes: Values, hopes, aspiration and Gender roles. The chapter highlighted how one's socio-economic background can play a crucial role in shaping their values, hopes and dream and influence the construction of gender roles in their minds. Drawing from the field of Marketing and other 11 official sources the chapter illustrated that values may be influenced by one's socio-economic status (SES), which in turn can influence one's motivation to act in a certain way. Differences in values can further lead to differences among couples or those who are co-parenting. One's SES can contribute to perinatal distress as the person navigate the question of becoming a mother/father during their perinatal period. Chapter 11 explored the major theme "History of previous diagnosis" and its two related sub-themes: Medical and Psychological of the Becoming model. The chapter drew from some of the latest research literature on this topic to highlight the importance of exploring the theme and its sub themes with perinatal clients. It also outlined the importance of paying attention to the intersection of chronic conditions, its impact on caring and the experience of exhaustion. Because these complex intersections can impact one's wellbeing during the perinatal period. Chapter 12 focused on risk assessment by exploring the major theme "Ongoing risk" and its related four sub-themes: Aggression/abuse/coercive control/domestic violence, Risks particular to socio-economic group, Nationality/immigration status and Religious/cultural. The chapter provided a list of major biological, psychological and sociological risk factors, focused on psychosocial risk factors and provided major definitions, prevalence and snippets from research literature and governmental sources relevant to the topics. The main aim was to emphasise the significance of risk assessment within the field of perinatal mental health. The final Chapter 13 explored the last major theme "Support system" and its four related sub-themes: Access to family/friends, Economic independence, Location (rural, suburb, neighbours) and Help at home (e.g., sleep/rest). The chapter illustrated the connections between these sub-themes and perinatal mental health. The chapter also provided rationale for the inclusion of these sub-themes and highlighted snippets of recent literature on this topic and definitions of the terms for the therapist's considerations.

In essence, each chapter has been a one-stop information guide providing a bird's eye view of the topics related to each theme and sub-themes. They are not meant to be comprehensive and are only meant as a starting point of conversation to have with clients or for the therapists to research these topics further. If there is any major take away from this book let it be this. Becoming a mother/father/parent is a journey and it is a problematic one. Some of us make it seem a smooth ride and some of us may have adventures on the way. As therapists, we are meant to not assume anything when working in this field. No matter how familiar we are with these topics and however amount of research we have carried out on this subject, each client and their experience will be unique. Hence as therapists working with perinatal clients, we must always examine our own presuppositions, assumptions and biases sitting in front of every client. Most of all, we must always stay curious and open to learning from our clients.

Index

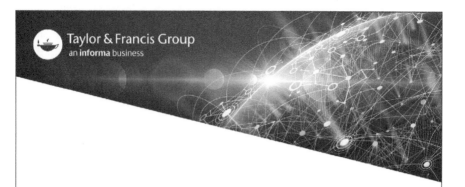